STATE OF THE HEART

State of the Heart

South Carolina Writers on the Places They Love

VOLUME 2

EDITED BY AÏDA ROGERS

FOREWORD BY MARJORY WENTWORTH

THE UNIVERSITY OF SOUTH CAROLINA PRESS

© 2015 University of South Carolina

Published by the University of South Carolina Press
Columbia, South Carolina 29208

www.sc.edu/uscpress

Manufactured in the United States of America

24 23 22 21 20 19 18 17 16 15
10 9 8 7 6 5 4 3 2 1

Library of Congress Cataloging-in-Publication Data
can be found at http://catalog.loc.gov/.

ISBN 978-1-61117-596-7 (cloth)
ISBN 978-1-61117-597-4 (paperback)
ISBN 978-1-61117-598-1 (ebook)

This book was printed on recycled paper with 30 percent
postconsumer waste content.

The old home began to seem like a human heart—generous,
understanding, unchanged by the years, wistful and thoughtful.
I began to feel that it is a terrible thing to love a place—if one must
leave it.

Archibald Rutledge, "I Leave Home"

Contents

ILLUSTRATIONS

FOREWORD *A Poem for South Carolina*

I take the role of poet laureate seriously; it is an enormous honor and privilege. During the eleven years I have served as South Carolina's poet laureate, I have used the status of the position to accomplish many important objectives, from cofounding a literary organization to serve the writing community and the greater community to reading handwritten poems by people who have written their entire lives and never shared their work with anyone. My goals have always been to increase literacy and literary awareness in as many ways as possible. This deeply honored position in South Carolina resulted in endless requests to speak at library openings, elementary school English classes, colleges, senior centers, and lighthouse and bridge openings. I have met so many extraordinary South Carolinians, and these connections have been a deep source of joy.

While the requests are unending, and most people assume it is my duty and my expenses are covered, during the last four years attending anything has meant paying out of my own pocket. Despite my efforts on behalf of the state, during the four years Governor Nikki Haley has been in office, I have received no communication from her or her staff on any matters and they cut my travel stipend. Perhaps it should have come as no surprise to hear that at Governor Haley's second inauguration there simply was no time for a poem. (Three minutes is not a lot of time my friends.)

Writing and reciting an inaugural poem is the one single requirement of a state poet laureate. At national poet laureate gatherings we discuss the inherent difficulties of writing poems for governors whose policies conflict with our own and the ironic fact that we often end up with a better poem because of that tension. Occasion poems are difficult to write: they have to work off the page and there can't be a lot of ambiguity. They also must be respectful of the occasion and not polemic. I was thinking about the poem for a long time and on December 4th I posted a request on Facebook asking the question, "What is your dream for S.C.?" I heard from more than fifty people regarding their concerns about improving our public education, embracing diversity and inclusion, and so on. One of the most extraordinary things a poem can do is to hold many disparate things together in a way that creates an entirely new meaning: one that only exists within the particular poem. "One River, One Boat" seems to be that kind of a poem. These disparate things are threads that run through my life but also speak deeply to others, and the response to this poem has been both moving and profound. South Carolina Congressman James E. Clyburn, who read the poem into the Congressional Record on the day of Governor Haley's inauguration, told me that everything he wanted to say about his seventy-six years on earth is expressed in the poem. An English professor from Arizona wants to name his unborn child after me. An artist and former Howard University professor wrote that the enslaved dreamed a poet like me would one day stand up for them and write something that holds up the mirror of truth.

These intense responses, and the media attention the poem received when it was cut from Governor Haley's inauguration, have to do with forces much bigger than I. The racial unrest that began in Ferguson and spread throughout the country in late 2014, coupled with the horrific killings at the Charlie Hebdo offices in Paris in early January that united the world in defense of free speech, form the backdrop into which the poem was dropped. It was a perfect storm of circumstances, and the poem resonated with many people who care deeply about social justice issues but don't necessarily have a voice. Isn't this the true job of the poet? I think it is, and I am so grateful for this opportunity to share it once again here as the foreword to this collection of essays by some of South Carolina's finest writers sharing their personal connections to—and visions for—our home state.

One River, One Boat

I know there's something better down the road.
  Elizabeth Alexander, *Praise Song for the Day*

Because our history is a knot
we try to unravel, while others
try to tighten it, we tire easily
and fray the cords that bind us.

The cord is a slow moving river,
spiraling across the land
in a succession of S's,
splintering near the sea.

Picture us all, crowded onto a boat
at the last bend in the river:
watch children stepping off the school bus,
parents late for work, grandparents

fishing for favorite memories,
teachers tapping their desks
with red pens, firemen suiting up
to save us, nurses making rounds,

baristas grinding coffee beans,
dockworkers unloading apartment size
containers of computers and toys
from factories across the sea.

Every morning a different veteran
stands at the base of the bridge
holding a cardboard sign
with misspelled words and an empty cup.

In fields at daybreak, rows of migrant
farm workers standing on ladders, break open
iced peach blossoms; their breath rising
and resting above the frozen fields like clouds.

A jonboat drifts down the river.
Inside, a small boy lies on his back;
hand laced behind his head, he watches
stars fade from the sky and dreams.

Consider the prophet John, calling us
from the edge of the wilderness to name
the harm that has been done, to make it
plain, and enter the river and rise.

It is not about asking for forgiveness.
It is not about bowing our heads in shame;
because it all begins and ends here:
while workers unearth trenches

at Gadsden's Wharf, where 100,000
Africans were imprisoned within brick walls
awaiting auction, death, or worse.
Where the dead were thrown into the water,

and the river clogged with corpses
has kept centuries of silence.
It is time to gather at the edge of the sea,
and toss wreaths into this watery grave.

And it is time to praise the judge
who cleared George Stinney's name,
seventy years after the fact,
we honor him; we pray.

Here, where the Confederate flag still flies
beside the Statehouse, haunted by our past,
conflicted about the future; at the heart
of it, we are at war with ourselves

huddled together on this boat
handed down to us – stuck
at the last bend of a wide river
splintering near the sea.

MARJORY WENTWORTH

ACKNOWLEDGMENTS

It's a pretty cool thing to be sitting in the hallowed South Caroliniana Library and come across your humble grandmother, particularly when she departed this life more than twenty years ago. But there she was, talking to me, so to speak, from the pages of a modest booklet put together by some of the students at Lexington Intermediate School, where I actually attended, albeit way more than twenty years ago. Those students had done what I never thought to do until it was too late. They interviewed Grandmama and others who'd been uprooted when Lake Murray was built in the late 1920s. So thank you to those students, and their teachers, Eloise Hiers and Ann Goldie, who had the foresight in 1988 to capture those voices for errant granddaughters and researchers who developed curiosity about that big event decades later.

Likewise, I must thank my aunt Cheryl Rogers, who came across a photo of my grandparents in front of the home they built on higher ground, and *didn't throw it away.* No, and she even made copies to distribute among the family. Because she did, I can see what my grandparents looked like when they were young. (This seems to matter as I get old.)

No book like this one makes it into print without the help of the story-tellers, the story seekers, and the story keepers. The writers who contributed their stories are all three; to each I send my deepest thanks and admiration. The same can be said for the artists and photographers who likewise contributed their talents. Several people across the state were pestered for images. I send warmest gratitude to Marion Haynes at the Horry County Museum; David Swanson and Jill Johnson at Newberry College; Melissa Moskow with Andrews's Old Town Hall Museum; J. R. Fennell at the

Lexington County Museum; Marie Peeples with the Barnwell County Museum; Daniel Harvey with the Barnwell County Chamber of Commerce; Bernadette Humphrey and Lisa Estes with the McClellanville Arts Council; Steven Strickland in Murrells Inlet; Kelly Evans with Blowfish Baseball; Father Stan Gumula, abbot of Mepkin Abbey; Helen Benso of Brookgreen Gardens; Sara June Goldstein with the South Carolina Arts Commission; Becky Hyatt Rickenbaker of Lexington; Emily Cooper of Asheville, North Carolina; and Women of Many Faiths in Columbia. Others helped with information: many thanks to Mary Bull at the Thomas Cooper Library at the University of South Carolina; Melissa Walker, Ph.D., at Converse College; Victoria Proctor, whose research can be found on SCIWAY; Dr. Bill Dufford, proud Newberry College graduate and supporter; Charlotte Gibbs of Aiken; and from Lexington, Reverend Dr. Patrick Riddle; Dr. Paul Austin; Commander Thomas J. O'Brien, United States Navy, retired; archaeologist Lonnie W. Franklin; and my aunt Azilee Lindler.

Beth Bilderback and Tracy Fredrychowski deserve spa vacations. Beth, visual materials archivist at the South Caroliniana Library, helped me secure just the right vintage photos. Tracy, a graphic designer and former colleague, advised me on current photographs. Both helped with volume 1; I'm shocked they don't run when they see me coming.

Several contributors to volume 1—remarkably generous the first time—helped in various ways again. Big thanks to Billy Baldwin, Lee Brockington, John Cely, Dot Jackson, Vennie Deas Moore, and Cecile Holmes.

My crew of sharp-eyed proofreaders are Cam Currie, Sharon Kelly, Amy Mann, Joy Simpson, and Diana Wilkie. They are the best.

Jonathan Haupt's name needs to be on the cover with Marjory Wentworth's and mine. The University of South Carolina Press, under his directorship, has supported this project in more ways than I can count. Because of USC Press, stories that matter are being told, and voices like my grandmother's are preserved and honored.

In her interview with those students, Grandmama talked about how she could hear her young children's voices echoing while they played in the pipes of the Lake Murray dam as it was being built. Sue Duffy wondered about those voices, those children and parents, who lived, worked, and played beneath the lake she loved so much. "Underworld" may be one of the last things she wrote before she died in June 2014. Maybe Sue, always curious, is talking to Grandmama now.

Finally, I must thank two of the greatest guys ever. Wally Peters always made sure I got bike and boat time when I needed it, and Hugh Rogers, my favorite English major, somehow was able to help me proofread manuscript pages in my mother's hospital room. He is my editor.

INTRODUCTION *Bittersweet*

Writers are magicians. Ask them to write about place, and they'll spin you a story about time, even if that time and place have misted into something else. But writers—God help us every one—can't forget those places. We puzzle over them, we ponder at them, and should we be asked to remember them in words, the temptation is just too great. The flood begins, the outpouring, of those people, those events, the smell of the air and the feel of the road, the tangibles and intangibles connected to one piece of geography that probably no one else would notice. Place, to writers, is so much more than that.

The writers who contributed to this book worked their magic on me, because after I read their stories, *I* went to another place. Not McClellanville, the quiet fishing village where I was hiding to work, but Lexington, the upright courthouse town where I grew up. Riding my bike around McClellanville, I seemed to be riding my bike around Lexington. It was almost like watching a movie, circa 1972. An empty-headed eleven-year-old is riding her bike around town, and she has her own circular route.

There she goes on her fuchsia Schwinn Sting-Ray, a backdrop of ranch houses and American cars sliding by. Up on the banana seat by the big Lutheran church, where so many of her friends are using a new word—*catechism*—in voices of awe and dread. Left by the big cemetery, and keep the brakes on. The sidewalk has cracks and goes downhill, and she doesn't want to miss her favorite headstone, the one with the ship. At least she thinks it's a ship, until she reads in her school book that it's a submarine, one named *Squalus,* and a sailor from Lexington was on it when it sank off the coast of New Hampshire in 1939. The story in the book was full of drama and fear—would the men be rescued?—but to her, it's even more of a thrill that the *sailor's brother's wife* is the gray-haired lady in the dentist office across the street, the one in the white uniform. It's too much to comprehend, this big, small world.

Deep breath at the bottom of the hill. There's a big intersection to cross, and she wants to get past the little store where her sister took a piece of candy and was hauled back to apologize and pay the penny. Uphill on the other side. It's the worst part, but the best part is coming. Pump hard by the post office, where her father taught her and her sisters over and over how to work the combination to open the box, and turn right. Main Street. And most important, the dime store, with its array of candy bars, lined up in boxes. They're so alluring, so tantalizing, she has to walk around the store a few times before she can decide which one to get.

It was a hard decision for that eleven-year-old, who never wondered where her dime came from, who didn't know that soon she'd need to look in mirrors before leaving the house, who couldn't conceive that one day driving a car on a different circular route would be much more exciting than riding a bike around town. Romanced by chocolate, seduced by commercials braying words like "nougat," she doesn't know—isn't capable of knowing—that life won't always be, as Donny Osmond croons on her record player, so "sweet and innocent."

I'd forgotten about that eleven-year-old, and her Saturday afternoon ride around Lexington, until I read these stories. And then I was back again, thanks to Ronald Daise, who's been chased, in a sense, by the live oaks of St. Helena Island to his workplace at Brookgreen Gardens. And Bernie Schein, who knows he'd be nothing without the good people in Beaufort who helped bring him along. And Margaret Shinn Evans, who found herself back in church twenty years after leaving all that behind.

I'm not sure you can leave it all behind, no matter how you try. Now, riding my bike in McClellanville, paying attention to the present, I see a place for children. In this village of shrimpers and artists, academics and renegades, there's a spirit of communal care for the young. "If somebody messes with our children," we're told, "you won't see that person anymore." And the children play without fear. In the summer, shirtless boys jump off boats into Jeremy Creek or fish from their own small boats. Girls, clustered with their iPhones, giggle and walk down Pinckney Street. There's a tree house with a captain's wheel, iron anchors rooted to yards for prospective Popeyes, and enough hollowed live oaks for legions of elves. Minus city pleasures, children entertain themselves.

Robert F. Gibbs, torpedo man first class, might have been looking for brighter lights when he left Lexington for the U.S. Navy in 1922. No doubt he found plenty that was new and different in Shanghai, where he was a submariner in the China Fleet. In Shanghai he met and married a Russian woman, was awarded the Yangtze Service Medal, lived through the Japanese invasion of China. But he wouldn't survive the *Squalus* disaster in New England, and his bride, with her broken English, would travel alone on a train from Lexington to Portsmouth, unable to understand that while thirty-three submariners were saved in an incredible rescue the whole world was watching, her "Bobbie" would be one of twenty-six who would not. "Only a little while dear, and I will be with you," his tombstone reads.

When you're young you see just the outlines of things, of ships that are submarines, islands that held slaves, roads along which oppressed people lived and worked and dreamed dreams. Your eyes have to change for things to fill in, become clear, find focus. Milania Gibbs came back to Lexington after waiting 114 days for her husband's body to be recovered from the cold Atlantic. More than two thousand people came to his funeral in Lexington, population reportedly 432, and flags were lowered to half-staff. Then Hitler invaded Poland, the Japanese attacked Pearl Harbor, and the *Squalus* story became a footnote. Decades would pass before the eleven-year-old would ride by and wonder.

Now she knows, and she wishes she'd known Milania. She would have said she's sorry. And offered a candy bar, because to her, that was the best thing in town.

Sea Turtle, woodcut by Anna Heyward Taylor.
Image courtesy of the Gibbes Museum of Art/Carolina Art Association.

Homing In

The large female turtle emerges from the nighttime surf and with great effort crawls to the dune line. She pauses. Then if satisfied with her circumstances she uses her hind flippers to construct a deep hole in the beach, and into this she lays her eggs. It is indeed awe inspiring to come upon one of these animals at its task, its breath sighing, eyes watering, body heaving. And on its back are bits of phosphorescent marine life blinking on and off. With luck a process has begun that will in the course of the summer lead to the next generation of loggerheads.

From *The Loggerheads of Cape Romain,* by William P. Baldwin Jr. and John M. Lofton. Baldwin was the junior refuge manager and Lofton the wildlife technician at Cape Romain National Wildlife Refuge when they conducted this study in 1939.

Nesting

Each spring my thoughts turn to the beach. Not to soak up the sun, surf, swim, or sail. In late May I await the return of the loggerhead sea turtles to Isle of Palms and Sullivan's Island. Sea turtles are ancient mariners that navigate the oceans until the voices of their ancestors call them back to the beaches of their births to nest.

From May to October, I join other turtle team volunteers to search the beaches for turtle tracks. I'm fortunate to be authorized by the South Carolina Department of Natural Resources to locate the turtle eggs, mark their nests with bright orange signs declaring them protected under federal law, move the nests to safe locations when necessary, monitor the emergence of hatchlings, and afterward inventory the nests for hatched and unhatched eggs and, usually to the oohs and ahhs of the waiting crowd, release trapped hatchlings to the sea. In other words I am a "turtle lady."

I began this adventure in 1999, when my sister telephoned from Florida to tell me how a sea turtle crawled up the beach outside her home and began laying eggs. Marguerite is an artist, and she described in colorful terms how the turtle cried great tears as she laid her eggs. Immediately metaphors danced in my head, and I knew I had to see this. The next day I became a sea turtle volunteer.

The first time I saw a female lay her eggs was a night I'll never forget. I was awakened in the middle of the night by a call from a fellow team member telling me to get there pronto. Her whispered voice was shaky with excitement. We never know when or where a turtle might come ashore, so seeing one is a matter of luck and God's grace. In high school I went to a Catholic boarding school where the nuns had us dressed and ready for mass in no time flat, so I'm a fast dresser. When I arrived at the beach, the loggerhead had just begun her trek toward the dunes. Breathless and wide-eyed, I hunkered down on the cool sand beside my teammates. We're careful not to disturb a sea turtle with noise or lights. If we do she'll turn around and head back to the sea without laying her eggs.

It was one of those miraculous nights when the tide was low and the full moon lit the pristine beach like an amphitheater. To watch a loggerhead's cumbersome crawl up the beach is to sit in awe of her courage and strength of purpose. She is slow and steady, contending with the unforgiving effects of gravity on her 350-pound body. I could hear the scraping of her flippers as she scarred the sand dragging herself along the beach, and her soft grunts when she stopped to rest. At last she reached a high point on the dune and went still. We held our breath.

Then the unmistakable sound of scraping began again as the sea turtle used her rear flippers to dig a nest some twenty inches down into the sand. We've discovered that turtles are less likely to be startled at this point so we moved as stealthy as ninja in the dark for a better view. Behind a clump of sea oats, we watched as she dropped over one hundred leathery eggs.

While she labored, I saw the thick streams of tears flow from her beautiful almond eyes. Science explains those tears as the natural excretion of salt from the eyes, but as a writer, as a woman, I saw them as a mother's tears. The tears of duty, love, and commitment. The tears of resilience and acceptance. She cries for her children, knowing all the predators that await her babies, the dangers of swift currents, the nets that can entangle them, the propellers that will slice their shells. I wept with her, thinking of my own children, knowing that all young are poised for leaving and that no mother can protect her children from their fates. We were just two mothers, having a good cry together. Perhaps that maternal instinct is why I was so moved when I saw those tears, why so many women vow to volunteer to protect the sea turtles, or have an affinity for the lone swimmers.

We watched in silence as the mother turtle covered and camouflaged her eggs. Then, without hesitation, without fanfare, she began the long, arduous crawl back to the sea, never to return to the nest. Each year as the season progresses and hatchlings start to emerge, we sit by nests like midwives waiting for the sand to move. When the hatchlings at last boil out from the sand we escort them to the sea as their turtle mother cannot. We call them babies, much to the chagrin of biologists, but that's what they are to us. Tiny, vulnerable, three-inch babies that follow their instincts and crawl in a comical frenzy toward the brightest light. In nature, that bright light comes from the ocean itself, glowing from its own phosphorescence

The author and hatchlings.
Photograph by Barbara Bergwerf.

and the reflection of the moon and stars. The sea becomes a nightlight for the hatchlings to follow home.

This model has worked well for more than a million years, but the advent of electricity has created a glare of light greater than nature's. For the turtles it's a false light that can produce nothing but hardship and disaster. Countless times I've watched with dismay as hatchlings dash toward the ocean only to turn away, confused, and head back toward the brightly lit streets and certain death. That's why we stay up by the nests, night after night, to redirect the hatchlings to the sea. We sit under the stars swapping bottles of bug repellent and stories. These women are not only my teammates, they're my friends. Like women have done for thousands of years, we gather for a purpose and are stronger for it.

It's always an introspective moment when I watch those tender three-inch hatchlings disappear into the sea. I worry if any of them will survive the perilous journey to the vast sargassum that floats in the Gulf Stream. I wonder if even one will survive the next thirty years to maturity and return to our beach to lay another generation of sea turtles. Only one in a thousand is likely to do so.

Yet I have hope. This summer I will begin my sixteenth summer as a sea turtle volunteer. I never would have guessed when I first started that these charismatic creatures would change my life and my career. At the end of a season, when the last hatchling makes it to the ocean, I stand shoulder to shoulder with my friends on the turtle team staring out at the sea. None of us speak. We don't have to. We are all lost in our own thoughts as we bid farewell to another season, to the mother turtles that are long gone, to the thousands of hatchlings somewhere out in the Gulf Stream.

As for me, I hope that in thirty years' time one of those hatchlings will make it back to the Isle of Palms or Sullivan's Island. I hope I'll still be standing here on this patch of beach, waiting to welcome her. The same way I welcome my children, grandchildren, and should it come to pass, my great-grandchildren.

This place is home to all of us. ☾

Barnwell Circle, painting by Beverly Hebbard.
Courtesy of Barnwell County Museum.

Our Town

Several towns in South Carolina have squares. Barnwell, though, has a circle. Surrounded by businesses and anchored by the courthouse, "the Circle" is where residents gather. As the Barnwell County website puts it, it's the "downtown heart of the city."

☽

A Saltwater Boyhood

I look back on my boyhood through a haze of memories. My earliest recollections of Myrtle Beach, South Carolina, evoke the smell of salt spray and the touch of beach sand, damp and cool against my bare feet. My world was bounded by the woods, a dirt road, and the Atlantic Ocean. Behind us were the woods; but Thirty-Eighth Avenue, unpaved until the 1950s, ran right by our house and two blocks down to the beach. My brothers and I made the beach our playground. I remember nights by an open window, listening to the surf rising in the darkness as my brothers and I tried to fall asleep in those hot nights before air conditioning. I was certain the sound of those waves held the secret of life. Some people believe the sea divides, but I knew somehow the sea unites. I knew that the waters that washed our shores connected me to people across the ocean whose shores were washed by the same waters. The coast, where the sea meets the land, is a good place to ponder connections: of sea to land, of nature to humans, of Europe and Africa to America, of tradition to change, of environment and economy to culture.

In those saltwater years I had vague and mostly mistaken ideas of what lay beyond the horizon, but it already inflamed my imagination. I used to stand at the edge of the sea and think, if I look hard enough, I can see England. But England is not directly across the Atlantic from South Carolina, Morocco is. And because I was peering toward a point exactly perpendicular to the slanting shoreline of South Carolina's upper coast, I was actually looking even farther south—toward Nigeria and Ghana.

My parents were part of that southern generation that grew up on farms and moved to town. At the end of World War II, we lived on Old Little River Road, just off Thirty-Eighth Avenue, in a house we rented from

Casper Benton. It is part of central Myrtle Beach now, but it was two miles out in the country then. Mr. Casper regaled us with stories about being the first man in Horry County to vote in the second grade. We laughed. He paused for effect, then hit us with his punch line: "Of course I wasn't supposed to be in the second grade. I was supposed to be in the *third* grade!" We roared, and then, with perfect timing, he hit us with his *real* punch line: "But they wouldn't let me be in the same grade with my Daddy!" He was the greatest storyteller I ever heard, bar none.

My brother Paul and I had to walk about a block down Thirty-Eighth Avenue to Highway 17 to catch the school bus each morning. If we could get there before eight we could catch a ride early and have twenty minutes to play basketball before classes started. Often we caught a ride with Robert White, a dignified and distinguished-looking man with white hair and white moustache. Paul and I liked his Scottish burr and wondered what brought him to Myrtle Beach.

I loved the music each Sunday at the First Presbyterian Church, about two miles south of our house. It was good that I did, for my attendance was never optional. In my family it would have done no more good to have minded going to church than to have minded heat in the summertime. But I loved the old hymns and the harmonies as we sang. I joined the choir in my early teens, as soon as my voice changed from my childhood alto to a deep bass. There I learned to read music—at least one line at a time.

Work was woven into our lives as deeply as religion. It may seem peculiar that the work ethic was so strong in Myrtle Beach, where so many tourists came to play. The tourist economy offered the opportunity—and the necessity—for summer jobs. Some folks in Myrtle Beach liked to say "they work us to death all summer and starve us to death all winter."

I was ten when I got my first job—a paper route. The summer after I turned twelve, I sold papers to tourists on Ocean Boulevard. That fall I worked in the print shop of our weekly, the *Myrtle Beach News,* owned by William A. Kimbel. Then I worked after school at the Thirty-Minute Laundry, until at thirteen I took a better-paying summer job as a grease monkey in the Myrtle Beach municipal garage. One of my tasks was to lubricate the police cars. A policeman complained that I missed grease fittings. I couldn't remember where all those grease fittings were. My father told me I didn't need to remember where they were; I merely needed to remember what they were there for. Wherever two pieces of metal rubbed together, I should look for a grease fitting nearby. It was a breakthrough for me from a world of education as memorizing to a world of education as disciplined thinking.

1940s postcard of the Kozy Korner in Myrtle Beach.
Courtesy of Horry County Museum.

I was able to extrapolate from the grease fittings the real meaning of his lesson: if I could learn how things work, I could figure out how to deal with them. It was perhaps the single most important lesson of my life.

At fourteen I obtained my driver's license and became a truck driver for the city during summers and on Saturdays during school. The pay was $41.25 a week—a man's wages—and I put $40 in the bank for college. I drove a dump truck north of Ocean Drive where Vereen's Marina was being dug beside the inland waterway. Several times a day I backed my truck down a long narrow fill to a dragline that deposited a mixture of sand and shell known as coquina into its bed. In Myrtle Beach in the 1940s and 1950s, we paved streets with this mixture. Although I came within ten miles of the North Carolina line several times a day for the next two years, it would not be until after I graduated from high school that I would see what lay north of South Carolina.

In the fall of 1951, my senior year in high school, I was employed by the Mid-Coast Real Estate and Investment Company, a partnership between George "Buster" Bryan and William A. Kimbel. I knew Buster because in earlier years, I babysat for his and his wife Marge's children. (As the oldest of four boys, I knew how to change a diaper, experience that brought me clients as a young teenager.) On Buster Bryan's recommendation I sat for Jimmy D'Angelo's children as well. Jimmy had spent the winters of 1927–29 as Myrtle Beach's first golf pro, at the Ocean Forest Country Club—today, Pine Lakes International. It was designed by Robert White.

White, a native of Scotland, came to the United States at twenty to study agronomy. He became a greens keeper and golf pro at country clubs in various parts of the country. By the time he began to *design* golf courses, he had educated himself in turf grasses, weeds, and watering, had learned how to design a green to make it drain properly, and how to shape a bunker to make it challenging to golfers. His unrivaled knowledge had a lasting impact on early golf architecture. Establishing an outstanding reputation as a club professional, greens keeper, club maker, and golf course architect, Robert White was elected the first president of the PGA of America in 1916. When he designed the Ocean Forest course in 1927, he was inspired by his youth playing golf on the seaside links of Scotland's "Auld Course" in his hometown of St. Andrews. The Ocean Forest course earned Myrtle Beach nationwide acclaim in the golf industry.

White worked closely with the actual builder of the Ocean Forest course—our landlord, Casper Benton. People now call that course "the granddaddy." In the late 1940s, he also constructed the famous Dunes Club course, which remains the Grand Strand's most famous design. His company, C. L. Benton and Sons, went on to build the Tidewater, Caledonia, and True Blue courses. *Golf Digest* has ranked each of these one of "America's 100 Greatest Public Courses."

Jimmy D'Angelo returned to Myrtle Beach year-round in 1949 to be pro at the new Dunes Club. For the next half-century he would be "Mr. Golf" in Myrtle Beach. His work as publicist and goodwill ambassador helped make the Grand Strand *the* destination for golf tourism. In 1954 he invited the National Golf Writers Association to a dinner honoring Robert Trent Jones, who designed the Dunes course. Thus began the Golf Writers' Championship, still held every year the week before the Masters. Jimmy D'Angelo was named a member of the Carolinas PGA Hall of Fame.

Buster Bryan's business partner, William A. Kimbel, was a member of our church, and I had worked for him in his newspaper print shop when we first moved to town. I did not know then that he had been a spymaster, director of Special Projects in the Office of Strategic Services (OSS) during World War II, or that the following year President Eisenhower would appoint him as a delegate to United Nations General Assembly.

My work with Mr. Bryan and Mr. Kimbel led to another job in 1952, one I would hold for the next six years. While the Myrtle Beach Farms Company actually owned many farms around the county, its main business had become resort development. It was, in fact, the company that first developed Myrtle Beach. My job was to count the money from the Myrtle Beach Pavilion, at that time the hub of Myrtle Beach.

In 1955 I took on an additional night job as box office manager of the Myrtle Beach Playhouse, a professional summer stock company offering mostly light comedies. Tourists and residents could see once-famous stars whose careers were fading—Veronica Lake, Sylvia Sidney, Robert Preston—as well as actors in the resident company whose fame later grew—Sandy Dennis, John Kerr, Robert Webber.

Even though it lacked many things we now consider necessities, I cannot imagine a better place to grow up than the Myrtle Beach of my youth. There was no hospital, no university, no library, no bookstore. But our one radio station, WMRA with its segmented format, offered more variety than all of them put together now. We knew fewer people with different accents, except in the summer; but we knew more people from different class backgrounds than now. And we lacked today's traffic jams (aside from the Fourth of July, and locals knew how to get around them).

I have lived, and still live, much of my life at the intersection of the academic world and the beach culture in which I was reared. Pondering that culture is more to me than merely a pastime; it is a passageway into the past. Echoes of "Good Rockin' Tonight" and "Sixty Minute Man" still reverberate in my ears and in my memory, growing fainter, sometimes barely audible, like a magical incantation, fusing the predestined and the contingent into something deeper than my conscious levels of thought and feeling. I am perpetually standing at the crossroads, at the same intersection between home and travel, between the conflicting tugs of my rootedness and my urge to ramble, that has preoccupied me ever since those long-ago days when I stood on the Carolina shore, gazing out across the sea and musing on my connections between myself and the world beyond the horizon. ʓ

The Soil of My Soul

Love is life and life is love. And both are friends of contradiction. Each romances happiness and hurt, while courting faith and fact. This is how I view my existence as a black woman rooted in the soil of South Carolina. The earth is rich and fertile here, but this was not always my reality. For me, my love for the Palmetto State has evolved as it became kinder to me and I forgave past pains birthed in a place now embraced completely by my heart.

As a black girl born in the 1940s and growing up in the 1950s and 1960s, I found there was little to love about South Carolina. My neck of the woods was Andrews. Back then, the South wasn't sold on multiculturalism and didn't celebrate diversity as we do today. Racial lines were drawn solidly in the sand and blacks stood on one side and whites on the other. Yet, I am the first to admit Andrews wasn't Selma, Alabama, or Jackson, Mississippi, both of which grabbed national headlines because of grievous injustices against the civil rights of people deemed too brown to be around those with white skin. Nevertheless Andrews had its way of making the souls of black folks weary. We existed but were considered invisible. And we knew that before Ralph Ellison's book was published. I knew the black man was the *Invisible Man,* while the black woman was just as invisible.

When I was eleven, I cleaned the homes of white families and learned that I, too, was invisible. White folks talked about me in front of me, as if I wasn't there. *The Help,* the book and movie, could have been set in the Andrews of old. Like those black housekeepers and nannies, we belonged to a dual reality mighty enough to break the spirits of the bravest among us. But we, the black children of Andrews, had our faith, our families, and a special secret weapon.

Joseph G. Thompson, principal
of Rosemary School. Photograph
courtesy of Andrews' Old Town Hall
Museum.

Rosemary School.
Photograph by Walter Shockley.

Rosemary School was a safe haven, and Joseph G. Thompson was the key reason. He was our principal, a fearless leader, who along with just enough empathetic teachers made certain we knew and celebrated our true worth. Mr. Thompson made sure each boy wore a tie to school every day. Girls had to dress like little ladies. Such simple directives were automatic self-esteem boosters. As soon as we crossed the Rosemary threshold, our confidence nearly outshined the sun. We straightened our backs. We held our heads high. We walked with purpose, and the invisibility cloaks came off. Seen and heard, we pupils were prized.

Rosemary wasn't the only place flourishing in Andrews. There was vibrancy in locales and locals unusual and expected. Main Street served up slices of the American Dream achieved by people white and black. Dunn's 5 & 10, a white-owned business, had the best chocolate-covered peanuts I ever put in my mouth. But the black establishments, like Rosemary School, kept hope for better days alive in my spirit. The McCrays, a black family, owned and operated a successful dry-cleaning business. They drove their vans to rural communities, where they picked up and delivered clothes to countless families. "Excellence" was their unspoken mantra, and they treated all their customers with dignity. By far they had the best dry cleaning business in town. I looked forward to the McCrays picking up my clothes earlier in the week and delivering them by Saturday so I could look fresh and fine for church on Sunday.

Mount Lebanon African Methodist Episcopal Church houses most of my memories of Andrews. My brother and I walked one mile to Sunday school each Sunday without fail. We eventually graduated to riding there on my brother's bicycle. James pedaled while I rode gleefully on the handlebars. In the choir my father sang praises, and to my ears, there was no sweeter music. Aged and unpainted, Mount Lebanon was its own clapboard miracle, producing joy and light for those inside. In 1952 it gave way to a house of the Lord fashioned from bricks. Now the latest version of Mount Lebanon bears my father's name, Wesley Tingman, in the cornerstone. It is a staunch reminder that my faith always had a solid foundation. There, in that sanctuary, we were connected, protected, and respected.

James and I spent wonderful, fun-filled summers at our grandparents' farm in Bonneau. We were packed weeks before it was time to leave. Being with our indulgent grandparents and their horses, cows, pigs, and chickens made us happier than a country cook eating collard greens and cornbread. The cherry on the pie was the staccato rhythm of the train passing behind their home. Its melodious clatter always came at breakfast. We listened intently and allowed our imaginations to soar. Where was the train going? What was on it? Who was the conductor? These moments were idyllic. The farm in Bonneau, and the pear, hickory, and oak trees we climbed, was our Garden of Eden. There, without serpents, tranquility reigned.

Still, there was longing. While Andrews and Bonneau embraced me, it wasn't enough to make me content. I knew a better life awaited me somewhere else. For southern blacks, the great escape was always on a north-bound road. That's why graduation day was our emancipation. We knew finishing our schooling meant heading to Reynolds Drug Store, where a long line of young black people patiently anticipated that Greyhound bus.

None of us had more than twenty dollars, and all of us had a shoebox containing lunch tucked securely under our arms. We were telling Andrews good-bye, carrying our dreams and those of our elders to destinations we believed were promised lands. My city of milk and honey was New York.

The Big Apple changed me forever. I became the woman I am there. I met the love of my life, who became my husband and the daddy of our babies, in that big city. I say, "I am a New Yorker," and I am unashamed to make that proclamation in company not too fond of "Yankees." But I am also a South Carolinian. I am a southern woman who has earned her stripes.

After decades in New York, I returned to South Carolina in 1995 and made a nest in Georgetown. The state's third-oldest city is tucked between the best of both worlds, Charleston and Myrtle Beach. The Holy City's breathtaking, historic homes alone are worth every drive, and the Grand Strand's festive atmosphere keeps me active alone or with friends. Wait, it gets better. I lucked up and found my piece of paradise on Belle Isle, a quaint community a rock's throw from Georgetown's historic Front Street. On Belle Isle, I wake up to nature. Birds in my yard serenade me. Their music is cooler than the compositions the roosters created to wake me during my childhood in Andrews, eighteen miles and about twenty-five years away. All of it is charming, though. I love just looking out my kitchen window and sitting on my front or back porch. I think of my property as a park, where the swing set resides for my grandchildren. A lone swing in the back yard is ideal for when I want to read a good book or the Good Book. Oh, how I love Belle Isle. The crickets and cicadas produce lullabies that put me to sleep like a freshly washed and powdered baby. It soothes me.

South Carolina has won me over. I see her without the haunting hurts, and she sees me. There's more beauty than blemishes. Nowadays, I bask in a simple, satisfying, southern life. I can play my life's soundtrack without skipping songs. Andrews, Bonneau, Belle Isle, and Georgetown are in heavy rotation. Each one takes turns playing, and each is a hit record with me. I trust South Carolina and I will continue making sweet music together. Tune in. ☽

☽

The Second Coming of Red Mitchell

My hometown of Beaufort, South Carolina, heralded by leading travel magazines as the loveliest small town in America, is home too to the Beth Israel Jewish Cemetery, a wrought-iron enclosed sunlit glade in which the souls of my parents float happily overhead among sun-shadowed oak leaves and softly glowing Spanish moss. Here at their gravesite, hand in hand in their adjoining graves, they're as delighted to see me now as they were in my youth, except, at least where Mom was concerned, when I had bad grades.

I wasn't the brightest bulb in the room, but I did, according to Dad, have "personality," which was true—I always got out of trouble by making him laugh when he was trying his hardest not to—but it was also his way of glossing over the fact that I was lazy as hell. Mom loved to touch me, to rub my back on the living room sofa if we were watching *Ozzie and Harriet,* or if it was not yet bedtime but I was sleepy. I feel her touch now, here at the foot of her grave. And Dad, he's at the toilet now making way for my brothers and me so we can all "take a leak" at the same time. "Why not, Boys," he'd offer, "we're all men"—particularly opportune, I realize now, when we were all fighting and clawing our way to the one toilet in the only bathroom in our house.

The brackish air from the Beaufort River, only a few blocks south, where we swam as boys and where the Gentiles fished and boated, often taking us with them, filled the cemetery with the fragrance of home. Yes, here I was home. I was home anywhere in Beaufort. My granddad, Samuel Schein, his wife, Esther, here beside him, in the late nineteenth century adopted a black infant abandoned on the Yemassee-to-Port Royal railroad tracks. A recent immigrant, perhaps he didn't know any better.

My dad's store, Schein's Grocery, is only a block or so from the cemetery. I grew up in that corner grocery store, in what is now called the Northwest Quadrant, but what was then called, at least by the whites, the slums, the denizens of which, mostly poor blacks and a few poor whites, were my dad's customers, "regulars." They were so kind and gentle, most of them, and often gave me a nickel, even when they couldn't pay Dad.

Back in the forties, Dad foresaw the war rationing of food, goods, and commodities. Above and behind the store itself he had rented rooms, mostly to marines from Parris Island, Beaufort's military base. In these rooms, now emptied out by the war, Dad stocked up on a surplus of goods, filling every available space with flour, salt, canned goods, household supplies, necessities which, as he predicted, became unattainable elsewhere. Soon those who were referred to back then as the "bigwigs," the monied and the aristocratic, the Country Club folks who shopped downtown, came calling, all hail-fellow and well-met.

"Sorry, Boys," my dad told them, eyeing, as they were, the magnificent stock spilling out of the shelves from top to bottom. "All this," he told them, "is for my customers, my 'regulars.'"

Here at his funeral in May 1979, I couldn't help but notice beyond the crowd and the wrought-iron gate black children walking past the cemetery on the sidewalk in their Sunday best, which I found curious, since this was a Saturday. Even more strangely, their black patent leather shoes were laced together, slung over their shoulders like pocketbooks. Will Myers, the son of the late Reverend Myers, a black friend not only of my granddad's but my dad's, to whose family Daddy and I used to deliver groceries on Saturday mornings, glanced my way, registering the quixotic expression on my face.

"Their parents," explained Will, "have instructed them to wear only their Sunday best today, out of respect for your father, and to take off their shoes since they have taps on the soles that go 'clickety-clack' down the sidewalk, and to tie them over their shoulders as they walk by the graveyard so as not to disturb Mr. Schein at his rest."

So many people, over the years, and the names here at Beth Israel so different than those on the gravestones in the St. Helena, the Baptist, the Presbyterian or Methodist cemeteries. There are no Joneses, Jameses, O'Reillys, or Harrisons here. No Chambers or Schepers or Willinghams or Cunninghams. No Harveys or Pringles or Danners or Washingtons. No, here at the Beth Israel Cemetery are the Levys, the Keyserlings, the Farbsteins, and the

Lipsitzs. The Neidichs, the Rudowitzs, the Hirsches, and the Rosenthals. The Rabinowitzs, the Liptons, the Marks—cousins—the Scheins.

There, a few rows over, is my great uncle David Schein, whose old dry goods store building, also on Bladen Street, the Beaufort Historical Society is now renovating. Mom told me that when Great Uncle David developed dementia, every Sunday morning he would pop over to the house and present Dad a check for one million dollars for having been such a good boy.

Perhaps because of protectiveness inspired by the Holocaust, or because there were so few Jewish children in Beaufort, or perhaps because of a largely unconscious yearning of our elders for lost selves wandering the waters and woods of assimilation, if you were a Jewish child of Beaufort, you belonged to the Beth Israel Synagogue, and you were adored by an entire congregation. To have the lovely Rose Mark beam at you as if you were her own was heavenly. To have Hymie or Josie Lipsitz turn and give you a smile and a wink while you were cutting up in the middle of the rabbi's sermon was deliciously conspiratorial. After I sang the Kiddush, the elders called me "little Eddie Cantor."

The rabbi wrote my entire Bar Mitzvah speech, and it was almost as bad as if I'd written it myself, but you'd have thought from the reaction of the congregation it was authored by Daniel Webster.

My mom made two requests for her burial, which was in October 2008. She was ninety-seven. On her gravestone she wanted a piano and a bridge hand. In front of me now are both. Bridge was her passion after Dad died, and she just beat hell out of everybody. She was a classical pianist who played for all synagogue events and to raise money for the United Jewish Appeal, for Israel, particularly in the post-Holocaust years, often performing with her sister, Dot Pearlstein, first-chair violinist for the Charleston Symphony for forty years. When Dot died in 1980, the rabbi from Charleston lamented "the quieting of the violin," yet Mom played on.

In her eulogy for Mom, my niece Vanessa reflected on one of Mom's reminders to her. "'Don't talk with your mouth full.'"

Mom particularly delighted, noted Vanessa, catching her in public.

"The beach, music, laughter, food. . . . According to Grandma, 'life's cure-alls.' . . . We were best friends, Grandma and I, sixty-five years apart."

Vanessa continued with her grandmother's advice: "'Work at having fun. Avoid eating all those greasy hamburgers and French fries at McDonald's,' which she herself would sneak off and do after every bridge game. 'Take care of yourself. Enjoy music. *Play bridge.*'"

"Thank you, Grandma," concluded Vanessa, "You played a wonderful hand."

My daughter Maggie spoke of Mom's last years, practicing and playing her piano to the end, "mostly deaf, her hands arthritic, gnarled with a perpetual cramp," marveling how "her fingers still knew the path" of a perfectly played Beethoven sonata, how "her heart dictated the rhythm," how "her soul still felt the way, her spirit resonating in the notes each time, becoming more and more clear, Grandma herself riding the exquisite waves, each note connecting to the other like pearls. . . . So Grandma," Maggie advised, "follow the notes all the way home now. Your soul knows them, let them carry you home. You have captured all of us in them: Granddaddy is there, your sister, your brothers, your sons and their families . . ."

The rabbi, to whom Mom was very close, marveled at the large turnout. He began delivering the Mourner's Kaddish when I noticed one head after another turning in the same direction in total disbelief. Red Mitchell, an old drinking buddy of ours who'd made a bundle off waste disposal, was sinking slowly—seemingly unaware so engrossed was he in the English

The Second Coming of Red Mitchell.
Illustration by Jonathan Hannah.

translation—into a recently filled-in grave of a person no one there but Rose Mark knew, until he was out of sight. About the grave's inhabitant, Rose said to me later, "serves him right. A retiree from New Jersey. Never paid his synagogue dues, only joined to get a plot."

During the burial ceremony, in which everyone lines up to shovel dirt into the grave, my brother Stanley's obsessiveness got the best of him when he couldn't stop shoveling and turn over the shovel to the next in line. When my younger brother Aaron intervened, Stanley got so excited that the last round of dirt went sailing into the crowd only to smack Red right in the face as he was climbing out of No-Name's grave.

Mom and Dad loved it. Everyone there did. Even the dead broke into laughter. And as we departed the gravesite and the cemetery through the wrought-iron gates onto Bladen street, they were still laughing, sitting up in their graves, shouting from one grave to another, visiting each other at their respective gravesites, on the common ground of the cemetery, telling and retelling the story over and over again. It was their story now. "Did you see . . . ?" "Did you hear . . . ?" ". . . Smack dab in the face!" And they couldn't get enough of it: Mom, Dad, the Levins, Dr. Keyserling who'd made house calls, Mr. Rudowitz who was president of the synagogue and so Old World and upright the locals called him Rebar, Hymie and Josie, our cousin Ernest Mark, Old LeRoy Keyserling who taught me how to sell a hamburger at my summer job at Pappy's Restaurant, Harriet Keyserling our state legislator, Mickey Lipton who sold us our first shoes, his wife, Cecile, who loved us with all of her heart, Bobby Hirsch who taught us how to spin dradles, the Farbsteins, the Neidichs, the Levys and Martin Levine and his wife, Sharon, of Martin's Men's shop, Cousin Meyer and Uncle David, all of them—husbands and fathers, mothers and wives, grandparents, children, all of them, laughing their asses off, at us, as we—Jews and Gentiles alike—got into our cars, reentering as we always did and as we always would, the greater community of Beaufort, our home, the loveliest small town in America. ☽

Penultimate Spartanburg

I'm near the end.

That is, deep into the last third of my life. At an age or in circumstances where, in the words of the actor Willem Dafoe (talking in a late-night interview recently about the meaning of his film *4:44 Last Day on Earth*), you become preoccupied—and occupied—with making amends and saying good-bye. The time when you may wind up doing what my father did near the end of his life: lie awake at night obsessed by the memory of all the perceived mistakes made, or sins committed, along the way (ironic since as a Presbyterian minister he had spent much of his life talking about and teaching forgiveness; and, of all the people I've known, he was the last one who ever needed to be troubled in such a way). The days when you experience the alarming cliché of seeing your friends and colleagues disappear one by one with greater and greater frequency. The age when the body starts to fail and the faculties diminish. To say these things is less complaint or lament than mere statement of fact and a nod towards our shared mortality.

I know, I know: it's the spiritual life we should be concerned with first and foremost at this point, with "our eyes upon eternal things" as we approach the end of our days, with that dimension perhaps best sought and expressed in formal, programmatic religious terms of prayer and meditation (I write this in the season of Lent, when those of us who have been shaped by Christian faith and practice are especially aware of the critical importance of the contemplative tradition). Those of this persuasion will also to the end of their lives be obsessed with trying to pursue social justice and human equity. But I find what I crave now is some vital expression of light and beauty—yes, beauty—and a bold, thoughtful embodiment of human kindness and good humor. Maybe the experience of these realities, or the search for them, constitutes the true spiritual pilgrimage for some of us in our final days and years.

The fact of our mortality, with its accompanying spiritual quest, leads directly to another fact. The fact of place, and its own begging of a basic question: where would you want to spend that last third of your life, those few remaining years? The final base or two from which to make amends and say good-bye? And find some light and beauty, human kindness, and affability along the way?

That question brings me to the small South Carolina upcountry city of Spartanburg, my next-to-last place of habitation on this earth.

In 2003 I relocated—I wouldn't say "retired"—to "Hub City" from Columbia, a place I dearly loved and where I had lived and worked for more than thirty years. But as I approached older age I needed to move "north" in order to be geographically closer to my children, who had established lives in Asheville. I did not want to leave South Carolina, because too many of my interests and activities continued to be tied to this state where my ancestors had lived as early as the eighteenth century in what is now Kershaw County and which had nourished me and my family directly since 1968. Spartanburg seemed to me to be the perfect place to relocate from Columbia. I had known Hub City and a few of its inhabitants off and on for more than thirty years, having been in and out of the town as field archivist with the South Caroliniana Library at the University of South Carolina (whose legendary former director Allen Stokes happened to be a native of Spartanburg). It seemed to be ideal both in size and in its proximity to Asheville. I could leave the front door of my condo behind the Jesse Boyd School on the east side of town and arrive at my daughters' in Asheville in a little more than an hour.

Right after moving to Spartanburg, I began to focus on claiming the "light" offered by its college communities—especially Wofford, Converse, USC-Upstate—and by those other cultural institutions and organizations whose members happened to respond immediately to my expression of interest in them. Principal among these, in addition to the new friends I made among the colleges' faculties and staffs, were the board members of the Hub City Writers Project and the Spartanburg Art Museum, then known as the Spartanburg County Museum of Art, and the personnel at the Spartanburg County Public Library.

Two other organizations have been key to my wonderful life experience here. The first of these is a handful of writers who dubbed themselves "Spoets" ("Spartanburg poets") and who, beginning in 2003, have tried to

The author/artist examines his work at the West Main Artists Co-op.
Photograph by Joan Wheatley.

meet monthly to read and critique each other's new work. This "family"
has included Philip Belcher, Aly Goodwin, Angela Kelly, Rick Mulkey, and
Nancy Taylor (from Greenville), all of whom during the first decade of
our existence have published prize-winning poetry. And then there is the
extraordinary phenomenon of the West Main Artists Co-op, initiated in
2009 by the indefatigable Howard Solomon and situated in an old church
sanctuary on West Main Street. The WMAC has proven to be a light- and
life-giving place for many of the area's artists, from strict amateurs to well-
known professionals. It has been another delightful community, a sanctuary where creative self-expression (for me, the shameless desire in my "last
chapter" to capture something of light, beauty, and humor on paper or
canvas) has been nourished and enabled.

Living in Spartanburg has also allowed me to be close to an additional beloved community that has claimed my time and interest in these final years: the Birchwood Center for Arts and Folklife in Pickens County. Its mission has been to salvage an ancient upcountry farmstead at the foot of Table Rock for use as a retreat and educational center and to undertake a variety of programs to augment the cultural life and preserve the environmental and folk heritage of the area. My fellow board members—from the Table Rock area of Pickens County and its spectacular Eastatoe Valley, Easley, and Anderson—are among the most astute, imaginative, hospitable, hardworking, talented, beautiful, down-to-earth people I have ever known.

Of course, the physical beauty has been everywhere around me in this territory, from the delectable views of changing skies and trees from my condo windows (among caring neighbors) to the handsome college campuses and the upcountry vistas of fields and woods in every direction from town, especially toward Gramling, Campobello, and Landrum, and along Highway 11. There is always the "heaven" of seeing the mountains rise in the distance a few minutes outside of Spartanburg heading north on I-26 toward the other Carolina. Whenever I make the trip in that direction, I think of the Old Testament poet who declared in what are among my favorite lines in the Bible (Psalm 121, RSV), "I lift up my eyes to the hills. From whence does my help come?"

I indicated at the outset that Spartanburg is my penultimate place of residence. For soon I must make one last jump: on up to that magic North Carolina mountain town whose most famous resident once declared "You can't go home again." Maybe not. But one can always seek to make wherever one lives home, that "last best place on earth"—that state of the heart meant to yield up its light and beauty, its human kindness and genial perspective. It may indeed be Spartanburg, where one finds himself living temporarily or penultimately (I have not regretted for an instant my sojourn here: it has indeed been my "Hub City," the hub of some of my best days on earth), or where one has lived forever.

Or it may be Asheville, where there is now the additional attraction of a toddling grandson. One last earthly home, an ultimate home, in which to continue to make amends and say good-bye. And live. ↄ

Rachel Haynie

Pride Goeth before a Fall—in Love with a Town

How dare I?

How dare any of us wear our places of origin like personal clan badges we smithed ourselves? We were infants, then children—too young to claim any of the credit due parents who brought us safely into the world, and baptized us in the font of a culturally rich town. We did not ask to be from Anywhere in particular—and yet where we're from shapes who we are, far beyond a name listed on a form asking Place of Birth.

Especially in the South, the brazen may ask first off and outright: "Who were your people?" while the unbrazen may ask instead, "Where are you from?" If the name you got from Your People happens to be recognizable, common to a town or area in this state, the nosy inquirers might just as well have gone on and asked to begin with: "Who were your people?" Past tense, see. Who your people Were. Because, to many, and in many parts of this state who your people were is still who you are. Maiden names can reveal what married names eclipse.

Beyond genetics and names, being from Somewhere is the first of many gifts our parents dole out to the ends of their reaches. For those of us lucky enough to love our hometowns, such love was, and still is, as much a fluke as whatever cosmic alignment attended our births, like love that flourishes in an arranged marriage.

My fortunate cosmic accident at birth has allowed me to keep saying, for all these years, that I am from Camden. Tenses in this, the state's oldest inland city, remain fluid.

When I was still seeing my world from the backseat window of a black Ford, the color choice Henry made available to all buyers, our family went for Sunday drives. On those afternoons I had pointed out to me the house in which George Washington slept when he stopped by in 1791. I was reminded the Lafayette Cedar, flourishing where planted on a congressman's home site at which the Marquis was entertained in 1825, honored the visiting general more so than his native France. We often ventured a few miles out in the country where the finger pointing was directed toward Mulberry Plantation, or as my parents called it, Mary Boykin Chesnut's house. I was fairly along in grade school before I figured out she wasn't there. And hadn't been for decades. I felt a little like I'd been fooled when I came to grips with her in past tense, but she was spoken of with so much regard I forgave the misleaders and moved on quickly to just wishing I could read her diary, and wondered if hers, like mine with a red plastic cover, had a little key like the one I relied on to lock my brother out of my girlhood secrets. All the while Mary's diary was in the public domain, shielded from no readers' eyes.

Knowing my town from birth afforded me a very different perspective than what outsiders have, especially outsiders who wish to become insiders. Then, some outsiders on extended visits to Camden brought with them a new verb, created from a noun. Was it the Chamber of Commerce or the news media that first referred to wealthy Northerners who stopped short of their November sojourns to Florida and decided instead to "winter" in Camden? Our sense of hospitality and welcome of whatever social and financial infusion they unpacked—along with their jodhpurs and golf clubs—called us to embrace them in spite of the certainty their ancestors had worn blue as surely as ours had worn gray. They made us their insiders when they allowed their children to play with us locals—after school—because the post-September arrivals of the Winter Camdenites relegated their offspring to keep pace in local private schools, an option that never would have crossed our families' minds.

Northerners' presence in Camden for a good part of each year made us appreciate our temperate weather, made us aware climate was a social magnet we had taken for granted. And knowing where these Northerners lived the rest of the year helped us realize there was somewhere else you could be from, and not always a town or city: you could be From Money. Well, some could.

They were different, almost exotic, so their return, about the time of first frost, seasoned dinner table conversation like a forthcoming election or weather phenomenon. Those who Wintered spoke more distinctly, wore their bearings most dashingly, had traveled more widely, so they held up a different mirror in which we regular Camdenites could view ourselves.

Pantheon to Confederate generals in Camden's Rectory Square. Courtesy of the South Caroliniana Library, University of South Carolina, Columbia, S.C.

The Wintering Northerners (our politeness protected them from being called Yankees) shifted the civic focus to the interlopers' lively activities, and slightly away from the dearly departed whose marble likenesses stood sentinel in the town parks, watching over our skating, sliding, and swinging. Early on, babies still in buntings and buggies were enveloped in Camden history merely by being strolled through sprawling public green spaces punctuated by monuments bearing sir names such as Kirkland, DeKalb, and Kershaw. From the top of the tallest downtown tower, Camden's children were watched over by patron saint King Haigler, the Catawba Indian chief whose forged-iron profile is a weathervane pointing the right direction.

In Rectory Square, one of the oldest parks, children—like me—disobeyed parents' orders not to climb on the Pantheon memorial. The warning was less for our safety and more a tutorial in reverence. As surely as we laid evergreen wreaths at family gravesites in Quaker Cemetery, we were taught to respect the civic heroes centering our playground. The six columns supporting the pergola stood, and still stand, for six Confederate generals: Cantey, Chesnut, Deas, Kennedy, Kershaw, and Villepigue.

We had it on good authority their blood had been shed for our freedom and probably had seeped deeply into Camden's sandy paths. Sandy sidewalks soaked up some of mine, too—shin-blood spilled when I went over my bike's handlebars.

Our heroes' blood lines had coursed through several more Camden generations by the time I recognized their names were still in current use by friends and neighbors, owners of local businesses, and a winning football coach.

We heard about the Revolutionary War in the same breath as the Civil War, so as children, we did not differentiate. We didn't know yet what dead meant, only that it deserved our respect.

There was so much civic pride and veneration in the references, I am embarrassed to admit: I was sitting comfortably near the back of a college history class when I was shocked by the professor's news that we did not WIN those wars! Cumulative perspective has helped me explain to myself how it was possible I did not know the Battle of Camden, the Battle of Hobkirk Hill, and the Great Unpleasantness did not gain us a single check-off in a Win column. Patriotism and honor were the reasons for my mistake.

I now understand pride is a double-edged sword: for defense and offense. Proverbs 16:18 admonishes us that Pride goeth before a fall. Too much pride, or false pride, can set you up for destruction. The other kind of pride, the kind that swells your heart, can set you up for a softer fall, a fall into love—a lasting love. With your town.

Like many who chafe against family bonds, anxious to leave and make a new path, I reached emancipation with customary high hopes. But going home I have always crossed that county line with a lighter heart, a mind dismissed of city worries. Back in Camden, I don't lock the car door—often leave the key in the ignition. I don't worry that being addressed as Ma'am is a salute (or affront) to my age as I do elsewhere, because there are still people who think of me as a young'un—Rachel and Everette's daughter. That's reason enough to drive thirty miles. That plus relatives and friends. I still have people. And memories that won't let go.

One is of Saddle and Paddle, the local swimming hole in a section of Old Factory Pond. Horses and dogs were allowed to cool off or be bathed there. My parents often took us for late afternoon swims after their full work days. To strengthen our confidence and swimming strokes, they would choose, from among a few cold-spring spots we all had memorized, a place where a stump remained about waist-deep beneath the surface. My father would swim out and stand on one, my mother would balance on another, and my brother and I would swim, first to one parent, then to the other; then back to shallow water from which we'd start over. Our two points on a triangle coaxed us into deep, then slightly deeper water. They were our buoys.

Someone to swim toward was an early form of goal setting. Long before my parents began swimming together, there had been in Camden many others whose distances and heights, opinions and achievements were worthy of targeting.

Your town can cause you to fall for azaleas and for horses that leave hoof prints along white-sand bridle paths, for monuments and magnolias that drop their cones for kids to use as hockey pucks skittering on concrete skating rinks. But behind all the love parading as pride, there are people. ☽

Family picnic, *Edisto Beach State Park.* Courtesy of the South Caroliniana Library, University of South Carolina, Columbia, S.C.

Family Beach Vacation

Hearken the roar of rushing surf
Or the dreamy lap, lap of tides,
Feel the din of the busy world fading away,
Let it go.

> Todd Ballantine, "Go to the Sea Like a Child,"
> *Tideland Treasure*

Cherry Grove Eclipse

In the late 1960s, my first wife, Carolyn, and I with our three children—
Ken the oldest, David a year younger, and Elizabeth four years behind—
vacationed for a week every summer with a modest rental house at Cherry
Grove Beach. That was right about the time it and three neighboring beach
communities incorporated as the city of North Myrtle Beach.

For years we drove from Columbia for summer vacation week. Ultimately, we bought a house that backed up on a dredged channel. On it
we had a floating dock. It took less than five minutes to walk to the Atlantic Ocean, near the Cherry Grove Fishing Pier, which for a half century
has been owned by the Prince family. Today it stretches behind the Prince
Resort condominiums, almost another five-minute walk into the Atlantic
Ocean.

Fall was the best season. Tailgating at Carolina home football games
quickly became a thing of the past. After Labor Day we'd get in the car
after work and dinner on Friday nights and drive three hours to the beach.
We regularly stopped about thirty miles out of Columbia for memorable
barbecue at Sikes.

In the fall the crowds were gone, the weather remained warm, and so did
the ocean until late October. Once tobacco harvesting ended, local black
farmers gathered to participate in a tradition no doubt brought over by
their ancestors from Africa. A few went out in small boats, laying out a seine
in a wide arc longer than a football field. Others waited on land, to help pull
it in.

The size of the catch varied. When the men detected large schools of
"spots" just offshore and heading south, a catch might well exceed a ton.
A small fish similar in appearance to perch, spots have a dark spot near the

mouth. On a big haul, fish were shoveled into a hundred or more wooden crates. But you could buy them still in the net, then placed on a hand-held scale to determine the price by weight.

The catch often included a few tasty Spanish mackerel. We'd buy several late in the morning and eat them with fried potatoes for lunch an hour later. Just thinking about it, forty years later, can make my mouth water. Other local men would catch sturgeon near the mouth of an inlet, which were brought in alive to a local entrepreneur. His crew deftly milked the females of their eggs and shipped them to New York for sale as fine American caviar to upscale restaurants. It rivaled imported Russian caviar.

At the beach, we regularly waded out into the surf, sometimes neck deep, for hours when the tide was coming in. When my children were small, one at a time would climb aboard an air mattress. My job was to catch a wave just as it was breaking and push them forward to ride just below its crest, sometimes all the way to the shore.

We also caught crabs off our channel dock, as well as shrimp with a throw net. With a small boat and motor, we could cruise out the channel into the tidal creeks to fish, catch shrimp, or just commune with the salt marsh. Late in the afternoon, we'd sit around on the back porch or deck, enjoying the sunset.

We developed a friendship with our next-door neighbor, a local farmer. I sometimes went out flounder fishing with him in his boat, stopping at his favorite spots in the tidal creeks. I would catch one fish for every three of his, but often still enough for a flavorful meal. He'd always add one or two to my string if he thought more were needed to feed a family of five.

Like everyone at the beach, we had our favorite seafood restaurants in Ocean Drive, the beach community just south of Cherry Grove. And occasionally we drove a few miles north on Highway 17 to Calabash, just across the North Carolina border. Over the years, we found a seafood restaurant that was special, at least for us.

Thanksgiving often marked the end of the season. Carolyn cooked a turkey, and we would drive to Sunset Beach, less than a half hour in North Carolina. We would walk on the beach to the isolated southern end of the island. There we would spread out a large quilt or its equivalent, everyone would get a plate, and we would enjoy a wonderful Thanksgiving meal.

For us the day after Thanksgiving was just as memorable. We held off on turkey sandwiches until Saturday, choosing roasted oysters instead. In our earlier years, we'd go to Horry's, a restaurant in Longs. Years later we pulled them from under our floating dock.

"I still long for oysters at Thanksgiving," my son David tells me.

None of us will forget the weekend at Cherry Grove when an eclipse of the sun occurred. I don't remember whether it was summer, but the weather was somewhere between warm and hot. We had studied how to view the eclipse by making a big pinhole in a spread-out cardboard box and looking at the sunny spot below on the sand. As the moon passed to block the sun, we all watched the small circle on the ground. The sky darkened and the air became chilly as the moon blocked all but the sun's outer skin. We experienced it all with a sense of wonder that would never be forgotten. My children, with children of their own, retain vivid memories of the awe of that once-in-a-lifetime (so far) experience.

Over the years we learned from a book we bought about shorebirds how to identify and distinguish the small sandpipers that would race across the beach on their tiny legs, the gliding brown pelicans that flew low across the water before diving into the surf for a bite of seafood, and the long-legged egrets in the marsh. A different book, about coastal flora, allowed us to know spartina in the marsh and distinguish across the range of plant life there and on the dunes.

My last visit to the house at Cherry Grove followed my marriage in 1994 to Nathalie Dupree while she recovered for a week from surgery. A threatening tropical storm cut our time short by a day, but by then I had followed her recipe for peach and blueberry cobbler. The directions were good and the cobbler even better. ☽

The Inlet in the Sixties:
How Cool Was That?

Ah, but I was so much older then,
I'm younger than that now.

    Bob Dylan, "My Back Pages"

I've always been fascinated by the concept of time. Every infinitesimal second of our lives we transition from past to present to future. Traveling from Point A to Point B on an endless ribbon, we weave our experiences into a single fabric. Dickens in *A Christmas Carol* described the past as "shadows of the things that have been." Time personifies these shadows, giving life to images imprinted upon our memories. They make our life canvas a work of Rauschenberg or de Kooning rather than scribbled graffiti.

The shadows of Murrells Inlet lurk in the apparitions of those who made it what it was and what it is: Blackbeard's marauding pirates, Bill Oliver piloting his steamships, legendary captains Alex Sing and Tommy Gaede guiding the *Thunderbird* dockside from the Gulf Stream, Maxine Oliver wielding a frying pan at Oliver's Lodge. Meanwhile, the Lees, Vereens, Dormans, Mayes, Morses, and Vaughts transformed a sleepy fishing village into South Carolina's seafood capital.

For me, shadows of pre–World War II Fords and Chevrolets rumble through Murrells Inlet, destined for Myrtle Beach. Back then Highway 17 was just a sketch on engineering drawing boards, and Murrells Inlet waited like some lowcountry Brigadoon. There it was, seeking refuge in its quaint and quiet past from an encroaching present and an apocalyptic future—one built on neon dazzle that would threaten the whole shebang.

On our Lexington County farm during the Eisenhower years, my family was fairly typical of the postwar South. Daddy had been a paratrooper in Europe during the war. One of seven children, he dropped out of Lexington High after Pearl Harbor to join the army, marrying my mother before basic training. Returning home after a brief stint as a Fort Jackson military policeman, he built a two-room home on an acre Mama'd been given by her father. The bathroom was out back. Our outhouse was the Cadillac of its genre, a two-seater whose memory is preserved by a flourishing scuppernong vine.

The biggest family event was our annual beach vacation. My father was a meat salesman for Roddey Packing Company in Columbia, and one of the job's perks was the huge station wagon he drove around the state hawking bologna, hot dogs, bacon, and sausage. It was a battlewagon, big as a Sherman tank and painted from headlight to bumper with Roddey red-and-white logos. It had large front and back seats with a vast storage area that would accommodate the entire population of Samoa and the Lesser Antilles. Roddey Packing Company, Mama's salary at Sessions Department Store in Lexington, and this humongous station wagon took us to Murrells Inlet for the first time in the 1960s.

Mind you, my sisters and I had never been anywhere. We'd go to Ray's Number One Drive-In every blue moon for Daddy's beloved John Wayne movies, but that was about it. Now we were going to stay at an honest-to-goodness beach house. How cool was that? And this was big: at the beach I would not have to endure Donna and Dale's endless slumber parties with their daft girlfriends (a bunch of girls running around in their pajamas, keeping me from my Saturday Night Universal Studio horror movies—what agony).

Most of the time when you rent a home, the residents leave the premises. That didn't happen at our Murrells Inlet hideaway. In fact, they would not leave even after we arrived. They stayed and made our lives miserable the whole week. Unbelievably, our house was infested with Catawba worms. Not just a few, not just a hundred, but thousands of creepy, crawly, disgusting yellow-and-black worms. I had seen Catawba worms (to some folks they're Catalpa worms) before. Daddy would buy them occasionally as fishing bait. I had just never thought of them as roommates. But they were everywhere—in our beds, in our hair, in the cereal, even in the Sherman-tank station wagon. We kindly asked them to leave, but they refused, stating they were there first.

Because our house was unfit for man, beast, or the Driggers clan, we fled each morning in the Roddeymobile, riding about Garden City, Surfside, and Murrells Inlet, making stops that would become our family traditions. I vividly recall setting out to visit a relative who owned Lakewood Camping Resort. Smack dab on the ocean, this place was a gold mine. There must have been a quadrillion RVs of all sizes and shapes in the place. Our own Daddy Warbucks had to be the richest person this side of Elvis. He was probably an eighty-seventh cousin thirty-two times removed, but Daddy treated him like long-lost family royalty. My sisters and I were in a virtual state of awe that anyone in our family, no matter how remotely kin, might be wealthy.

Alex's Marina was another must-visit. Captain Alex specialized in hauling folks to trawl the Gulf Stream. Daddy relished watching the catch of the day paraded before admiring dockside crowds. Conversely, my sisters and I enjoyed the spectacle of departing seasick passengers in various shades of blue. Once Daddy spotted one of my mother's mother's brother's sons working on the fishing boat baiting lines. His father had large business holdings, and upon his death, these considerable properties were distributed to the family. Translated into liquid assets, these meant that this particular son would never have to work the remainder of his life. But there he was at Alex's, baiting fish on a fishing trawler. Although frittering away a fortune, Mama's prodigal cousin had no regrets. Like a Kerouac character, he eschewed the conventional for a Dean Moriarty-ish open road. Daddy, a product of the 1930s, couldn't understand it. I was a creature of the 1960s and did understand, at least as much as the Lexington version of my Haight-Ashbury sensibilities allowed.

The following day, the Roddeymobile hit the road for a round of golf. Not the Dunes Country Club, the layout at Augusta National, or the course at Pebble Beach. My sisters wanted to play wacky golf. Myrtle Beach is to miniature golf what Mick and Keith are to the Rolling Stones. One simply cannot exist without the other.

It seemed every square foot of frontage on Highway 17 between Murrells Inlet and Calabash teemed with plastic icons embodying Andy Warhol, Bugs Bunny, and John Waters's unconventional vision of mid-century America. My sisters and I chose a particularly fetching, and thoroughly tacky, prehistoric course replete with fifteen-foot synthetic molds of T-Rex and his dinosaur kin, and vast watery concrete lagoons. Dale, who hadn't

Bay Harbor Restaurant.
Photograph courtesy of Murrells Inlet History Project.

the foggiest notion about which end of the putter to strike the ball with, ambled to the first tee and swatted her drive through the mouth of a plastic T-Rex, down and around its tummy, out through its tail, and into the hole. It was a miracle worthy of the book of Genesis, a stroke to make Arnie and Jack proud. Dale was elated; Donna and I were dumbfounded.

Born that afternoon was our tradition of wacky golf. That evening a new tradition took hold—supper at the Bay Harbor restaurant. I have to believe there's something imbedded in the human genome that requires our species to return to the same nooks each year. At home we never ate out. Never. Our annual pilgrimage to the Bay Harbor became our big night out.

Across the street from Alex's Marina, the Bay Harbor restaurant was descended from the Bay Harbor Hotel, which opened in 1945. Its royal lineage of ownership included Mac and Teeny Oliver of Oliver's Lodge fame. You could never go to the Bay Harbor without having to wait for a period of time that seemingly exceeded that of the Woodstock festival. Still, the wait was always worth that moment of high rapture when you finally entered the holy of holies, the dining room, to see, smell, and partake of the mounds of fried oysters, scallops, and clams. It was a feeding frenzy nonpareil.

The Bay Harbor closed many years ago, but it was always my restaurant of choice in Murrells Inlet. Subsequent pilgrimages brought others—Oliver's

Lodge, Russell Vereen's Seafood Grill and Raw Bar, and Jimmy and Kim Mayes's Inlet Crab House. It's a shame unsuspecting tourists flood to those 1,473,812-item buffets on Highway 17 selling seafood cooked when Truman was in office at a cost per plate of the national debt of Peru. Murrells Inlet was, and still is, the seafood capital of South Carolina.

My father died in 1974, shortly after returning from his last vacation to the beach. He was only fifty-two. My memories of him often center on our trips to Murrells Inlet and the Carolina coast. I can still see him in T-shirt and Bermuda shorts, wearing a cooter shell hat, sitting on the porch of our rented house grappling with a five-thousand-piece picture puzzle. My mother still talks about the time we and the Cromer family almost drowned on the Intracoastal Waterway when a sudden storm enveloped our boats. I remember driving our centuries-old jeep across the sand dunes with my sisters, herky-jerking a manual transmission none of us knew how to operate, and our trips to Pirate Land. Those trips were documented on 8 mm film Daddy shot on his Sears and Roebuck camera.

Mama and my sisters, we still have our photo albums. And I watch those old family movies every coon's age. Has it really been fifty years since we were the guests of all those Catawba worms in Murrells Inlet?

The older I get, the more I cling to memories. And the more I realize how much I've been given. My parents gave me an education they couldn't afford, braces they couldn't afford, eyeglasses they couldn't afford, and discipline and love that endures.

Shadows travel along time's conveyor belt from past to present and are tugged by my heart along life's pathways. That's something no house of Catawba worms can ever take away. ⌣

Girl with Watermelon on Her Shoulder Near Manning, S.C., by Marion Post, Farm Security Administration. Courtesy of the South Caroliniana Library, University of South Carolina, Columbia, S.C.

Farm and Garden

I am a farmer's daughter. . . . Whenever someone says, "tell me about yourself," I start my story with the farm and the farmer.

Melissa Walker of Spartanburg, "One Foot in Each World," in *Black Earth and Ivory Tower: New American Essays from Farm and Classroom*

Vera Gómez

☽

Avocados Are Always Ready to Use

Maybe it's the eighty-nine-cent-per-pound blood-red ripe tomatoes in the blistering heat of an August afternoon. Or the varied shades of green visible in the slope of iced-down heads at a dollar and nineteen cents a bunch. The romaine, the green leaf, red leaf, and iceberg are all mixed in the refrigerated section at the back of the store. The greens sit tall. They are perched among the picked herbs, parsley, cilantro, mint, and fennel, nestled near the broccoli, leeks, and beets.

Maybe it's the people. The hushed commingling of voices from under the hum of summer's oscillating fans or the drone of space heaters in winter's silence. At the Tomatoe Vine in Greenville, I heard my first hint of Carolina, and the voices and grit that weighed on the pages of Dorothy Allison's work came to life. From the "ma'am" and "mister" I hear from Dee at the checkout to the "si" and "no" I hear from the stockers, I adore my weekly run to this local farmers market. For me it's about more than bounteous, affordable food. It's about what it represents: yesterday and today, the old with the new, Southern gentility with hipster hip and the best produce around.

The first time I went there, I needed real Hass avocados, ready-to-use avocados. I'd been invited to a cookout and was asked to bring my guacamole, a party favorite in the circles I run in. Typical me, I waited until the morning of to go to the market. After looking everywhere and hopping grocery chain to grocery chain—Harris Teeter and Winn Dixie were contenders back then—I called one of my oldest friends in Greenville. LeeAnna, a "native" as she often reminds me, simply said, "Did you try the Tomatoe Vine on Old Buncombe?"

That first visit, I stepped through the side bay door onto the coolness of the concrete floor. After my eyes adjusted to the dim light, I walked around, surveying this market that didn't look like much and will never compete with the trendiness of Greenville's Saturdays Downtown Market. Still, the Tomatoe Vine has authenticity, evidenced by its array of produce and in the people who've shopped here since the 1970s. Then it was a small roadside shack that a former Cash n' Carry employee started because he wanted to sell locally grown vegetables, LeeAnna's mom, Nancy, told me.

Sam Staggs owns the Tomatoe Vine now. He added an "e" to the word so people would remember the name. The first owner, Charles Manley, named it Country Garden Curb Market, and it stood at the site of an old 7-Eleven. Charles added to the building as his produce business grew, and Sam bought it in 1997. A garden grower since he was a kid, Sam helped his family farm two hundred acres. At one time his grandfather, Troy Melton, was one of the largest peach growers in South Carolina.

Produce is in Sam's veins. Besides being a lifelong grower and wholesaler, he's an entrepreneur. When NAFTA opened up trade in 1994, he decided he needed a second location to grow his business. Yes! My Tomatoe Vine is actually licensed as the Tomatoe Vine II. The first was on Highway 29 in Greer.

Why go? Because you can find ginger root, yucca, and purple potatoes, and Suber Corn Meal and Amish jellies made in the Carolinas. If you need banana leaves to wrap a pig for dirt-pit cooking or affordable fruit for a party tray (still the best prices in town), you come here. This is where I found serrano peppers before any of the big-box stores carried them. It's also where I've purchased cut aloe vera leaves to use as a salve, dried corn husks for tamales, tamarind soda (a throwback to my parents' Mexican up-bringing and my tonic when homesick), and the largest jicama to salt and lemon for dessert.

Besides produce, the Tomatoe Vine is rich in stories. A wrecked racing car panel, Number 37, hangs across the rafters opposite the front doors. Sam drag raced for a while and sponsored the car. Mud-wrapped wasp nests, found elsewhere and posted here, look like old-man noses attached to the wood beams. The smells of dried tobacco leaves and boiling peanuts hint there's plenty going on in this simple, off-the-beaten-path market I found in desperation and now patronize so frequently.

For me the Tomatoe Vine transcends time. It is calm, a realm apart from the hectic corporate supermarkets and the fashionable Saturday morning downtown scene. Here, in front of the tomatoes, is where my poem about

The author examining tomatoes at the Tomatoe Vine.
Photograph by Steve Marlow.

my father's battle with cancer and last days in the hospital came to me. The words spilled into my brain as I held the blood-red fruit:

At the farmer's market
I hold one to my nose and smell the earth
We got paid thirty bucks a day
to pull tomatoes—orange, red and green,
even the heirloom ones in all of their deformity.
When my father started his garden,
I'd tend to it. Water, weed then push
past the leaves to grab the fruit.
Once in my palm, I'd yank it from the vine.
By late summer the heavy ones hit the ground.
Their skin split, their seeds spilt.
If the stink bugs had not invaded I'd salvage them.
I took tomatoes to Dad's hospital room once,
where with his pocket knife cut it open and let it bleed.
Salting the flesh,
I brought a slice to his lips
and let him taste the earth.

Sure there are grander and prettier places. Caesar's Head, Paris Mountain, the bridge at Falls Park. But it is here among the wooden stands and the flies in summer and crisp cold air in winter that I hear and see the South. White, Black, Hispanic, Asian.

My favorite spot inside the Tomatoe Vine is the "ugly table." It's hidden from view, near the canned goods at the right of the front doors. When you pick items from it you need to tell Dee so you'll get the discount. For me the ugly table holds the best among the bruised. Picking through the soon-to-be-tossed peppers, apples, oranges, and eggplants, I've met the most interesting Carolinians and have had the warmest conversations. It's where I pick the best, already ripened tomatoes to throw in with the Hass avocados that are always ready to use.

Vera's Guacamole Recipe
3–4 ripe Hass avocados
1 medium-ripe tomato
1 medium purple onion
1 lime (will use half)
Dash of Mrs. Dash
2 twists of sea salt (from grinder)
2 splashes of Texas Gunpowder

Slice and dice the tomato and onion, mix into medium-size bowl. Halve the avocados and remove the pits. Using a tablespoon, scoop each half on top of the tomato and onion. Do not mash, do not mix. Once all avocados are scooped, add Mrs. Dash, sea salt, and Texas Gunpower (my first secret ingredient). Keep one pit and cut the lime into quarters.

With a knife and fork, cut into the avocados like you're cutting a steak and fold over the tomato and onion. Repeat this step 3–4 times, squeezing the juice of a quarter lime into the mixture and making sure the avocados stay chunky (this is the second secret along with TLC).

Once finished, use your spoon to flatten the top of the guacamole, then insert the pit and squeeze the last quarter lime onto the top of the mixture. Top off with a splash of sea salt. Eat with tortilla chips or solo. ☽

Jim Casada

☽

A Love Affair with the "Angry Ann"

Growing up in a rural setting closely connected to the land provides a sense of place and a need to be rooted to the soil. Native land lays hold on a corner of your soul, or at least that's always been the case for me. Most of my fondest memories from childhood onward revolve around life lived close to the good earth. Fishing for trout, hunting small game, hoeing corn, helping my grandfather slop hogs and feed chickens, lending a hand at hog-killing time, picking blackberries and dewberries, gathering poke "sallet," catching night crawlers and salamanders to sell to bait shops, and myriad similar activities filled my youth with a full measure of simple pleasure. Adulthood has brought wider horizons and greater opportunities—I've hunted and fished all over the world—but the underlying importance of "connectedness" to the land has never changed. I long ago realized the truth in the historian's adage suggesting "you can't know where you are going if you don't know where you've been."

Coming from a family that for generations knew and loved the land gave me, at an early age, a sense of linkage to the good earth. That helps explain why my personal commitment to the American dream—a family, my own home, staunch adherence to the Protestant ethic, and a deep-seated belief that there is something edifying and uplifting about work—also always included a fervent desire to own a decent-sized piece of land. I wanted sufficient acreage to provide opportunities to call back vestiges of yesteryear. To live in a fashion where earth and its offerings served as a sort of mental umbilical cord, a stabilizing influence providing a place of escape where I could relive my boyhood and vicariously touch hands with those stewards of the land who formed generations of my predecessors.

That mindset defines my favorite place in South Carolina. Although it is at a considerable remove from my native heath in North Carolina's Great Smokies, my little farm was acquired because it lies close to where I have lived for more than four decades, offers me a place to hunt and be at peace and frankly, because it was affordable. It also has natural features: a grove of black walnuts, a pawpaw thicket, wildflowers, and two branches that carry me straight back to my boyhood. Members of my family laughingly call the farm "Angry Ann Acres," the name my son-in-law gave the tract. That was because initially my wife was, shall we say, less than wholeheartedly enthusiastic about the realization of my long-cherished dream. Thankfully she has come to realize, over time, just how much this little piece of land means to me.

To the average observer, my hundred acres in Chester County is nothing special, but through the eyes of this hopeless romantic it takes on a dream-like aura of delight. It's a place for roaming in the gloaming, for wondering while wandering, and for indulging in soul-soothing respites from the realities of a fast-paced world. It's where there's quiet comfort in being reminded that daylight and first night are wonderfully different in the country and where welcome intimations of self-sufficiency, realistic or not, afford a way of looking back to life as it once was lived. To me, such things are of the utmost importance, although I would hasten to add that they are better understood in person than in print.

Viewed from a practical perspective, the tract that has become home to my heart might be considered an ecological laboratory for the negative aspects of King Cotton's reign. Its hilly portions, sloping down to a pair of branches, show evidence of devastating erosion. But nature's healing hands have long since smoothed those scars etched by mindless monoculture with a mixture of mature hardwoods—beech; white, willow, and scarlet oaks; hickories; and other species. Thickets of undergrowth mark other portions, logged perhaps two decades ago and shortly before I acquired the land. This is gradually yielding, year by year, to pines and gums, which, as they grow, deny the smilax and sedge, brambles and browse plants, the vital sunlight they need to survive. Bottomland portions along the brace of branches are populated by elms, sycamores, dogwoods, redbuds, a sizeable canebrake, and appreciable stands of black walnuts, a species my grandfather styled the "three generation tree" because it is so slow-growing.

This woodland diversity has its intrinsic appeal, thanks to providing mast for wildlife, nesting places for wild turkeys and songbirds, cover for cottontails, bedding grounds for whitetails, high-rise homes for bushytails, and fertile hunting ground for foxes as well as this writer. Having such a place, one where I could hunt at leisure and not worry about other club members, poachers, or the "pumpkin army" of orange-clad whitetail enthusiasts drawn to public lands each autumn, formed the primary reason for the original acquisition of what locals call a "farm," never mind that the only real crops being raised are game animals and trees.

Early on though, as I walked the land, familiarizing myself with old roads and boundary markers, pausing to ponder at an old homesite or admiring the initials of lovers carved into a beech a half-century ago, realization dawned that this land would reward me with much more than hearty meals of venison or uneven April battles of wits with lordly gobblers. Those things were important to me and continue to be so, but increasingly hunting became but one part of a much larger whole.

Discovery of scattered patches of morel mushrooms, an early spring bounty demanding careful searching, an observant eye and knowledge of

Morels growing on the Angry Ann Acres. Photograph courtesy of the author.

the kind of conditions conducive to the fungi's growth, translated to feasts few folks in this part of the world enjoy.

Two large patches of pawpaws meant that in seasons where late frosts didn't kill the blooms there was promise, come fall, of enjoying George Washington's favorite dessert, pawpaw custard. Even if the pawpaw crop failed or 'possums and 'coons beat me to this oft-overlooked delicacy, there were persimmons to provide the makings of that most scrumptious of sweets, a persimmon pudding. Blackberries growing along trails and in an old logging yard begged to be picked in June, while the abundance of black walnuts cried out for gathering, drying, removal of hulls, and tedious yet wonderfully rewarding cracking for their meats to be used in cakes and cookies. In short, the ability to harvest earth's abundant wild bounty through the seasons and in many forms moved and mesmerized me.

As surely as my love affair with this piece of land deepened and diversified, my desire to call it "mine" strengthened. It engendered an ownership desire sufficiently strong to produce several years of feverish endeavor. Besides writing articles for outdoor magazines, there was a spate of ghostwriting, considerable editorial work and consulting, and a general extension of my efforts as a full-time freelancer. In less than a decade the mortgage was paid off, the candle no longer had to burn at both ends, and a simple son of the soil could now take quiet pride in land ownership.

It's that sense of accomplishment, that ability to realize the dream of a lifetime, that makes this acreage in Chester County so special to me. It sustains my soul and awakens my senses in so many ways—as a hunter and a gatherer; as an enchanted observer of wildflowers; as an audience of one listening to the chorus of the wilds as nature greets a new day; as a connoisseur of delicate wildwood aromas wafting on thermals at sunset; and most of all as someone who is still a boy at heart, now trapped in an old man's body. To know such joy on land I can call my own, even if only for a brief span of a few years, is to tread trails of wonder on the backside of heaven. ☽

Clam-Stuffed Morel Mushrooms
10 medium to large fresh morel mushrooms, sliced in half lengthwise
⅓ cup butter, melted
1 garlic clove, minced
1 (6 ½ ounce) can minced clams
3 tablespoons finely chopped green onions or chives
1 tablespoon finely chopped fresh parsley
Salt and pepper to taste

¾ cup mayonnaise
½ tablespoon prepared mustard

Clean mushrooms well and remove stems. Cut in half lengthwise. Chop the removed stems finely. Melt butter, add minced garlic and mushroom stems and sauté for 8–10 minutes until stems are tender. Drain clams and add to skillet with onions, parsley, and salt and pepper. Sauté for 5 minutes. Stuff morel halves with clam mixture and place in a greased baking dish. Combine mayonnaise and mustard and top each stuffed morel half with a dollop. Bake for 10–15 minutes at 350 degrees. Serve immediately.

Blackberry Cobbler
1 cup all-purpose flour
1 cup sugar
2 teaspoons baking powder
1 cup milk
½ cup (one stick) butter, melted
2–4 cups blackberries

Combine flour, sugar, baking powder, and milk; stir with a wire whisk until smooth. Add melted butter and blend. Pour batter into a 9" x 13" baking dish. Pour berries (amount depends on whether you like lots of berries or lots of crust) evenly over batter. Do not stir. Bake at 350 degrees for 30–40 minutes or until golden brown. Serve with vanilla ice cream, whipped cream, or milk.

Note: This recipe works equally well with a number of other berries including dewberries, raspberries, elderberries, huckleberries, and blueberries.

)

Love Me, Fear Me

I hope that one of the things the people I love find most endearing about me is my ability to fill them with fear. My husband, who still shakes his head in wonder when he sees my delight at knobby truck tires pushing through wet clay on a dirt road, feels it whenever I hear the Call of the Country. Suddenly his prissy-looking wife is demanding to load the kids into the car and drive toward nothing in particular.

Aaron's biggest scare came fairly recently when I discovered that an old, storied property called Grovewood was for sale in Eastover, adjoining land our neighbors own. The Call of the Country bounced off the walls of our already chaotic house for a good three months while my obsession reached levels many psychologists would find worthy of study. I had an entire plan laid out for our "weekend house." Never mind that it's only been a few years since the idea of buying the house we currently own would have seemed preposterous. Never mind that Aaron spends the majority of his free time on airplanes headed for meetings, conferences, and research symposia. I knew how I was going to make that 250-some-year-old property into a creative sanctuary for this family, come hell or high water.

Somehow, we didn't end up buying Grovewood, and while our home is a bit more peaceful for it, I'm still waiting for the day that my eyes don't get moist when someone mentions its historic name. For once my ability to frighten didn't win.

I think the first time I ever truly scared my parents was when I found the horse farm. I was in the seventh grade and hated where we lived. The brick ranch my parents had settled us into upon our quick move to Orangeburg, South Carolina, from Racine, Wisconsin, two years before represented a

Eastover hayfield.
Photograph by David Hartfield.

world both foreign and hostile. A too-good-to-pass-up offer from a small-town hospital landed us in a gangly, awkward house on the only dirt road in a distant subdivision. We always emerged dusty, but my parents didn't seem in much of a hurry to find a better—or at least cleaner—house. Still, I scoured the Columbia newspaper's classifieds every time I could get my hands on them. I wanted out of that neighborhood. I wanted nothing to do with the kids who taunted me for my huge glasses and preference for my bike and books over them. I wanted to share space with the horse my father had gotten me in an attempt to purchase me a friend. That purchase was his first mistake. I'd never experienced the bond of horse ownership, and Mr. Hitch, an ornery dark bay Thoroughbred, became my snarky BFF.

One day, in the sloppy sanctuary I'd created out of my room, I came across an advertisement for a farm in Eastover. I called the name listed in the advertisement—a man who would later go into hiding after telling a syndicated radio show that the Confederate flag should fly everywhere around the world as a symbol of hope. The voice on the other end kindly humored a precocious child. Later, he called my parents to make sure the appointment was real. They were all so tickled they decided to go with it.

What we didn't know is that the thick, horsey air of Eastover is like an addictive drug. One stroll through a hazy yellow field and any fantasy you've ever had about living an idyllic country life will return and overtake the frontal cortex of the brain. If there's any possibility of purchasing the field you're standing in when this happens, you're screwed. I'm fairly positive that's how Eastover's old families, the Westons and Hamers among them, came to reside in one of the most beautiful places to exist in the middle of nowhere.

Eastover thoroughly intoxicated my parents our first few years there. My father would have to drive along cloaked, alligator-haunted roads for forty minutes to get to Orangeburg's Regional Medical Center when he was on call, but that was a happy, solitary time for him until the late-night nature of the drive became too much for his patience and stamina.

One of the things my parents missed most about Wisconsin was their social life. Parties would pop up in our living room when friends or neighbors got job promotions, sold works of art, got married, got divorced, or sneezed. A couple of years ago at LaGuardia airport in New York, I noticed the man next to me staring at me with a puzzled look on his face. It was Vernon Jordan, the prominent attorney and civil rights activist, and he'd been present at one of my parents' shindigs when I'd been skipping around in my flannel nightgown, probably doing the Richard Nixon impersonations that were my bartering chip for staying up late. Mr. Jordan probably was staring at me because there was food on my face, but in my mind he was trying to figure out if I was that same kid—not because I'm exceptionally memorable, but because my parents' Wisconsin parties always were.

As soon as we moved to Eastover the parties started again. The quiet air and inky nights seemed to create a communal feel, as if the strangely loud croaking of bullfrogs triggered the telling of secrets that didn't flow as easily in a city. There was also the novelty of a black family having purchased a plantation in South Carolina, which often brought curious visitors to see if the rumor were true. Sometimes we'd look out our kitchen window in the morning and see strangers sitting in john boats in our pond.

On any given weekend, my friends and I dangled our spindly legs in the pool, licking the remains of ice cream sandwiches off our fingers. Depending on the number of visitors, a pig could be roasting behind the barn, surrounded by old men from Eastover who'd spent many years staring at engines and smoking Marlboros. Cackling from fancy-swimsuited adults would burst randomly through the pool house screen. Our house may have been a third of the one we'd left in Wisconsin, but part of our normalcy had returned. Except now that normalcy included fishing off a dock and participating in the work required for a twenty-eight-stall horse training facility.

Not having fabulous wealth meant plenty of manual labor for us. My mother ran a tight ship, making sure all shrubs were perfectly mounded and azaleas trimmed to best show their droopy pink splendor. Summer brought zillions of peaches and plums, and we had to figure out what to do with them before rotting brown flesh attracted more flies. My mom, never a good cook, kept our freezer chest full of really terrible peach cobblers. For a while, every dish had something to do with those fruits.

Seeking advice for fixing old trucks, my dad got to know Eastover's slow-moving, tight-lipped elders, who usually spit tobacco and grunted instead of offering advice. There were two trucks, but on a good day only one worked at a time.

When the hayfield was cut I joined the hired hands at the barn, tying and tossing hundred-pound bales into the storage loft. Once I could legally drive, those days would end with a run for soggy barbecue sandwiches, salty cracklings between the grease-soaked bread and smoked meat.

I don't remember exactly when my parents decided it was too much. I do remember the melancholy that seized me the day we moved back to Orangeburg. I was a junior in high school, prone to spontaneous fits of faux anguish and melancholy, but this time the melancholy felt real, as if it could drape the shoulders of everyone who came near me. On our final trip from the farm to our new house, my parents were in a tiff over how much time it was taking to finish clearing out. My mom was driving—doing her version of speeding, which wasn't much to speak of—down Highway 601, annoyed with my dad for pushing her to hurry and with me for filling the passenger seat with teenage angst. As the Cadillac went around one of the route's many blind curves, a little white terrier ran across the road to a woman and two children jumping up and down, calling for their sweet dog. There was nowhere to go. No time for my mother to even move her foot from the gas to the brake.

Later, as we both sobbed, I thought—and quite probably said—that we never would have killed that puppy if my parents hadn't sold the farm. I saw it as a cruel sign that my parents had made the worst decision possible, and now the world was falling apart because of it.

Of course that wasn't true. My parents weren't equipped for life in the country and had already moved on in their minds. But there's still a part of me that feels the tickly itchiness of tall, sunbaked grasses at certain times of the year, something like the phantom sensations of an amputee's lost limb. The time hasn't arrived for me to incorporate Eastover into a few sections of my life, but I think it will one day. Perhaps without having to scare anyone. ꙮ

Katie Stagliano

Miracle of the Cabbage

When I was nine, my priorities were slightly different from my priorities now as a teenager. Racing home from school to play with friends was high on my priority list. Ending world hunger? That had not exactly crossed my mind. I was oblivious to all of the problems that riddled the world. Unicorns and fairies were still real, and I still did not like eating my vegetables at dinner.

However, something happened one day in February of 2008 that would literally change my life forever. Three tiny green leaves sprouted from a brown peat pot I'd planted in a sunny spot in my back yard. I'd received a cabbage seedling from the Bonnie Plants 3rd Grade Cabbage Program, which was started to inspire a love of vegetable gardening in young people across the country. That seedling was my catalyst!

Those three tiny green leaves grew into a life-changing, enormous cabbage. Just how enormous? Ginormous, nearly the size of my four-year-old brother. I was astonished that my little cabbage seedling had reached such a hefty size in a mere three months.

Every night before dinner, my father would tell us how lucky we were to have a healthy meal on the table every night, because there were some families who go to bed hungry and rely on soup kitchens for what could be their only meal of the day.

One night, as my father was telling us how fortunate we were, I looked out the window of our Summerville home to see my huge cabbage. I had been struggling with what to do with it for a while, but at that moment, the answer could not be clearer. I was going to donate my cabbage to a soup kitchen where it would help feed all of the families in need who rely on soup kitchens for what could be their only meal of the day.

With the help of my parents, I located an amazing soup kitchen. And one morning in May, we hauled my cabbage to Tricounty Family Ministries in North Charleston. It was so big we had to put it in the back of my dad's SUV.

I will never forget the reactions of everyone standing in line for a meal as we pulled up to the driveway and carried the cabbage in. They gasped, and I received countless hugs from people I had never met, thanking me for everything I had done. I heard people whisper, "Is that for us?" and "She's so kind to donate that to us."

I had no idea such a small action would spark such a huge reaction. And though I was just bringing one cabbage to feed these people, they made it seem like I was giving them something much greater. The smiles and hugs made the experience even better.

At the door of Tricounty, I was greeted by the incredibly bubbly and kind "Mrs. Sue" Hanshaw. She gave my family and me huge hugs and then proceeded to make an even bigger deal about the size of my cabbage than the guests outside. She insisted we weigh the cabbage on the big scale in the storage room. After my dad set my cabbage on the scale, we learned it weighed an impressive forty pounds. I was completely blown away. Never in a million years did I, at nine years old, think that I would grow a forty-pound cabbage.

Mrs. Sue insisted I draw a silly face on the cabbage before it was taken to the back. After drawing the silliest face I could muster, the volunteers took my cabbage to be cooked. The head chef explained it would be turned into cabbage soup, with ham and rice served on the side.

I was invited back to the soup kitchen that Friday to serve my cabbage, which would become several giant aluminum pans of cabbage soup. Friday could not come soon enough for me. When I arrived, I was greeted with the same enthusiasm as when I had brought my cabbage. I sat between two other volunteers with my giant plastic gloves on and a large ladle to serve my cabbage. The guests would walk through a covered porch and pick up their food at a window.

All I could see from my side of the window were faces, and all those faces wore smiles. I saw so many faces that day, and so many of those faces were kids, just like me, walking through the line with their families.

A couple of days later, I received a letter from Mrs. Sue. She thanked me for donating my cabbage and told me I had helped feed 275 people with my one cabbage. Thanks to Tricounty Family Ministries, I had a completely new perspective on soup kitchens and hunger. Hunger had a face. And I had seen 275 faces of hunger that day.

Katie and John Michael Stagliano with the "Cabbage That Changed Everything."
Photograph by Stacy Stagliano.

Tricounty Family Ministries is my favorite place in South Carolina, not only because of my experiences there, but because of all of the incredible people who made that day even better. The hugs, smiles, and praises from the guests of the soup kitchen, Mrs. Sue, and volunteers gave me the greatest feeling of joy. It left me with the feeling that although I was a child, I could make a difference in the world. That day, I knew that by donating my cabbage, I had made a difference.

Since then I've been growing and donating vegetables to Tricounty Family Ministries, and have even started a garden there so they can grow their own fresh produce too.

What happened at Tricounty was life changing for me and for kids across the country. That day my dream to end hunger, one vegetable garden at a time, was born. I founded Katie's Krops, the not-for-profit organization whose mission is to start and maintain vegetable gardens and donate the harvest to people in need, as well as to inspire others to do the same. Children across the country are now growing Katie's Krops gardens and supporting their local soup kitchens, just as I supported Tricounty. And the dream of that little nine-year-old girl grows on. ☽

Pear and Cabbage Salad
1 small red cabbage, cored and thinly sliced (about 6 cups)
5 pears, cut into thin slices
1 carrot, shredded
½ cup golden raisins
½ cup extra-virgin olive oil
¼ cup balsamic vinegar
2 tablespoons honey
½ teaspoon salt

Place the cabbage, carrot, pears, and raisins in a bowl. Whisk vinegar, honey, salt, and olive oil and drizzle on top of the salad. Toss and enjoy.

George Singleton

Strange Love in a Small Pasture

If you go to one of those satellite images via computer, and zoom in on the pasture at the corner of Thomas Mill Road and Hester Store Road— the fenced ten or so acres adjacent to a two-story stone house, across from the vacant two-story stone general store—in zip code 29640, you'll witness where this sad, relentless tale took place. This is Dacusville. Easy weepers beware. I don't usually think of myself as nostalgic, prone to cry, or melodramatic, but in September of 2010 I slowed down near this particular intersection, witnessed what occurred, pieced it together correctly, and felt my heart wither more so.

Now, at times I've been known to be hyperbolic and, on good days, comedic. What I have to relate here is neither funny nor exaggerated. It involves a trailer fire; some bartered rabbits; a horse and pig that once lived apart; my good ex–auto mechanic Dean Nash, who lived a half-mile from me in the stone house and came down with MS in his mid- to late thirties; and a deaf woman.

The old sway-backed mare was named Candy. The pot-bellied pig was named, unfortunately, Blackie. At one time Blackie lived with a family inside their trailer, across Thomas Mill Road from where Candy slowly grazed around in her pasture. The singlewide caught fire, the pig ran across the macadam, scooted beneath the split-rail fence, and, evidently, pig-trotted his way to the horse. A few days passed, as days do pass for burned-out trailer-dwelling people focused on retooling their lives, before Blackie's owners returned to the area to search for their pet.

There stood Blackie, portly and bottom-tusked as ever, *beneath* Candy the horse. "Come here, Blackie," the trailerless people called, or something like that, according to Dean Nash, my ex-mechanic. These people walked forward toward their traumatized porcine trailermate.

Candy the horse whinnied hard and—maybe for the first time in years—reared up on her hind legs. She rotated her fetlock joints like one of those kung-fu masters warming up.

Dean had come out to witness this event, which paralleled some kind of Capulet/Montague scenario. The trailer people—now long gone from the area and uninterviewable—backed off. The man said, "Hey, do you want to buy a pig?"

"No," Dean said. "Well, I guess I can trade you something for it. You want some rabbits I raise?"

Dean used to build engines for NASCAR drivers. If I were prone to hyperbole in this particular essay I would write, at this point, how my Jeep could go 160 miles an hour because Dean Nash bored out whatever it is engine builders bore out. My old Jeep might hit 80. There seems to be a problem with the air conditioner, something my new good mechanic Johnny finds mysterious.

The man took the rabbits. Candy unreared herself. Blackie stood beneath her. By "beneath her" I mean "the pig mostly stayed directly beneath Candy's sagging belly," especially during rainstorms, for twelve years.

Now, whenever people came to my house for the first time, my directions went something like this: "Turn on White Horse Road and drive four miles. You'll cross the Saluda River. You'll see a life-size plastic bull in the front yard of some people with no landscaping tastes. At the intersection of 183 and Thomas Mill Road, take a right. Take the first left—you'll see a horse with a pig underneath it—onto Hester Store Road," et cetera.

Dean got diagnosed with multiple sclerosis in the late 1990s. It got to where he couldn't climb the stairs in his house, and he put it up for sale. He folded up his mechanic shop out back and sold the house, the shop, his land, and Candy and Blackie. Part of the deal involved the new owners taking care of the horse and pig.

So for a dozen-plus years nothing changed when I gave people directions, at least up to the pig beneath the horse part. I should mention that, over the years, a new church sprouted up in a Butler building next to the pasture, a whole trailer park showed up behind where Blackie's first owners' trailer burned down, a field behind the old stone Hester Store got developed into a number of 5–10-acre tracts, and so on. A Clock's Original Drive-In opened, and a Spinx gas station. There's a Christian Ladies workout place that opened and closed, and a chiropractor's office, and a suntanning place.

So then it happened that I drove home at dusk and saw Candy on her side, Blackie standing next to her. A veterinarian, Dr. Derek Wessinger, knelt at Candy's head. Her heart was giving out. "It was the most remarkable thing I've ever seen," he told me later. "That pig was talking to Candy, and laying against her. The pig was frantic, nudging her, pulling on her tail, then going over to pull on her mane. It was more than I could take, I tell you."

Candy had to be euthanized, finally. They placed a blue tarp over her body until she could be taken away. Blackie slept next to her. My better half, Glenda, called the next morning on her way to work, crying, and said, "That tarp blew away in the night. Blackie's right up against Candy's stomach."

My next-door neighbor, a pediatrician named Angie Millon, has horses and hires out Dr. Wessinger. He had told her that he worried about Blackie, and a couple months after Candy's death Angie asked that I go see if maybe the pig's owners would let her adopt Blackie, so he could return to the equine world. I went over there—I'll talk to anyone about a horse and a pig, of course—but I'm not sure that Blackie's owner understood me, for she's deaf. She did tear up as I talked about seeing Candy on the ground, so I guess she knew why I showed up unannounced at her abode.

Within a month or two, a black Labrador retriever and a Chihuahua—I'm not lying here—began palling around with Blackie in the pasture. At one point I'm sure you could've looked on Google Earth, found an obese pig, a Lab wearing a red collar, and *a dot,* standing in a field, off the corner of Thomas Mill and Hester Store roads.

Listen, I've told this story to a number of people. They say it would make a great children's story, except for the trailer fire, the MS, and the death of the horse. Children, it appears, don't deserve the cruelties of love. And of course it gets worse: I drove to work one day and came across a dead bobcat, ten feet off the road, nearly up against the fence where Blackie lived. I got out and nudged the thing—it was a beautiful specimen, and by the afternoon a traveling taxidermist had evidently happened by—and thought to myself how I hadn't seen Blackie, or his new friends, in a while. Because I took logic in college, it didn't take much to piece together what had more than likely occurred.

I have never gotten the courage to go ask the deaf woman whatever happened to her adopted pot-bellied pig. I can't take seeing people cry when good memories crop up over barnyard tragedies.

Unfortunately, I don't foresee these scenarios occurring much in South Carolina in particular, and the South in general, presently. We won't see

Candy and Blackie living together. There will be a Starbucks in the pasture. No one will ever have to drive by, see the saddest friendship this side of *Animal Farm,* and cry. It will not be a better existence, in my opinion, for any of us.

As an aside, when I first moved to the area in 1992, a man drove a horse trailer filled with llamas up to some gas pumps at the local Texaco convenience store. I stood behind a man at the register wearing cutoff jeans, no shirt, and no shoes. He looked out the window for a long moment, turned to me, and said, "What the hell kind of donkeys is them?"

I've since moved to Spartanburg County. No matter. I still have my Dacusville. ◡

Julia and Bill Rogers, Lexington County.
Photo courtesy of Aïda Rogers.

Lake Murray

"I'd never go back to those days. I don't ever want to go backwards. I've adjusted, and it's O.K. now."

Julia Harmon Rogers (1898–1993), who with her husband, Bill (1895–1966), moved their farm in Lexington County to higher ground in 1928 when Lake Murray was formed. This photo, taken around 1944, shows the couple in their "new" home, built from the timbers of their old one.

From *Memories of the Lake Murray Dam,* by the EAGLE (Enrichment Activities Geared for Exceptional) students of Lexington Intermediate School, 1988

⟩

Underworld

The old man closes the front door of the house where four generations of his family have lived. There's no need to lock it. In a short while, it will all be under water. He crosses the porch and pauses on the front steps. Spread before him is the broad Saluda River valley, where he spent a lifetime farming, fishing along the riverbanks, and carrying his family to church, where the whole community gathered to worship and share Sunday supper.

Now that valley lies barren before a massive new dam spanning Dreher Shoals. Whole forests have been toppled to accommodate it. Most of the homes downstream have already been destroyed, their gardens hastily harvested and left to drown. His church is torn down, and though there's talk of rebuilding it on higher ground, its cemetery holding the remains of his parents and grandparents will be lost to the coming flood.

One of the last to evacuate the valley before the now-harnessed Saluda backs its waters beyond its banks and onto his land, he takes one last look at his ancestral home and walks away.

He is the embodiment of the five thousand people who lost their homes, livelihoods, and way of life in the late 1920s. Far beneath the surface of Lake Murray are whole communities, schools, churches, a bridge, and cemeteries that sometimes reappear during draw-downs of the lake—all sacrificed for the common good. South Carolina needed more electricity for its growing population, and the gushing power of the Saluda was tapped as the source. Today the dam—completed in 1930, the world's largest earthen dam at that time—and its colossal 2005 backup dam hold back 763 billion gallons of water that fill a basin covering more than forty-eight thousand acres.

When my husband and I moved to Lake Murray in 2000, I didn't know that the bones of another world lay scattered on the lake bed just beyond

Red Knoll School at its 1917 dedication.
Photograph courtesy of Lexington County Museum.

our back door. Not just the submerged villages settled by the Germans and Swiss, but the trails and settlements of the Cherokees who harvested the river and hunted its valley, leaving behind the stone-honed tools and arrowheads lake dwellers often find on their beaches today.

So what do I think about when we ride our Jet Skis over the lake's cobalt waters? How far down is the old man's house? Is the submerged bridge that once spanned the original river bed still intact? Where were the schoolyards where children played Red Rover and Pop the Whip? Am I passing over them this moment?

There is one place I'm sure of. I was there when a piece of Lake Murray history was raised to life after sixty years in a cold water tomb. In 2005, about two miles west of the dam and 150 feet down, divers worked for days to secure the crippled B-25 bomber that had plunged into the lake during World War II. Just a year after the Pearl Harbor attack, Colonel Jimmy Doolittle had come to Columbia Army Air Base to assemble and train the B-25 crews that would soon launch a retaliatory air raid on Japan. The famous Doolittle Raiders practiced their aerial attack on Japan by dropping flour-sack "bombs" on one of the lake's uninhabited islands, which we now

B-25 rising from Lake Murray in 2005.
Photograph by Jay Schabacker.

call Bomb Island. During one run, though, a plane experienced mechanical failure and ditched in the lake, its crew surviving the crash. That plane was about to surface again.

Once contained, the plane was dragged at a slow crawl just below the surface of the water to a waiting crane on the north side of the dam. Hundreds of people lined the dam and crowded about the steel cradle waiting to receive the aircraft. It was one in the morning when the mangled warbird first broke the surface, and a hush fell over the still-gathering crowd.

As the plane slowly lifted from the water, one elder gentleman near me pulled himself up straight and saluted the lost warrior that had finally returned from duty.

Its hydroelectric power in less demand now, the lake is a playground. Its 620 miles of shoreline are built up with homes and docks anchoring all manner of watercraft, but not one single B-25. On a Jet Ski, though, you can squeeze into backwater sloughs where 1920s cabins and farmhouses still sit on high ground, saved from the onslaught of the Saluda. I cruise slowly behind them and wonder what it was like for their earlier inhabitants to watch the valley below them disappear in the flood, or hear the roar of Doolittle Raiders massing for their historic air strike.

Lake Murray's a storied place. Its waters sparkle like pavé diamonds, its sherbet sunsets radiant upon them. But its depths are the keeper of murky mysteries and a decaying history. It's best sometimes to turn off the Jet Ski and let the quiet rhythm of the water drift you into another age, one that begs to be remembered. ☽

The Long Lake View

I grew up in central Kentucky, a land abundant with ponds, streams, rivers, and lakes. I spent my childhood wading through the algae-slick creeks of my grandparents' farm where hills folded down into rich bottomland. Most days, I could be found turning over flat shards of limestone, capturing creatures that dared live within my grasp. Like any country kid, I knew all the local critters—crawdads, minnows, snake doctors, water skaters, hellbenders, and a newt species we called water dogs.

I learned to ski in the blue waters of Green River Lake. At three, I was atop my father's shoulders, my legs wedged tightly under his arms. I struck a fancy posture like the ladies in the logos on our Cypress Gardens skis. My father leaned into the roiling V the boat churned out. He pulled hard against the rope, his muscles clamping down on my ankles as we picked up speed, my heart in my throat. We cleared the trenchant waterline with a solid smack and then there was nothing but the hiss of our skis kissing silky water outside the wake.

When we were considering where to move, my future husband showed me Lake Murray. He knew my attraction to water, and I'm sure he felt it would close the deal both on moving and marriage. As soon as we settled into Columbia, I found the local ski club and made friends with other adrenaline junkies. They were a fun group, and we often camped on the islands in the middle of the lake. Frog Island was a favorite, but we were troubled by the sizzle of toads (not frogs) that hopped into our campfire on their way to the water's edge each night. We drunkenly built barricades to route the little guys away from the flames, but there was still the occasional pop and somebody always proposed a toast to honor the fallen.

After about a decade, we bought a funky octagon-shaped house on a hillside on Lake Murray. At the top of the lake, on the Lexington/Saluda county line, the spot was idyllic. There's no other way to put it. I've been to more South Carolina beaches and historic towns than I'll ever be able to recall. I have spent a number of weekends camped in the Blue Ridge Mountains after whitewater rafting the Chattooga, where James Dickey's novel *Deliverance* was made into a movie. But the placid murk of Lake Murray will always have a special place in my heart.

The Lake House was all we ever called it. No cutesy name. No wooden sign beside the door like the beach houses of our adopted state. We had a few pieces of bad fish art on the walls. A steep path scattered with wild violets and red velvet ants descended to a double-decker dock where we kept an enormous 1970s twin-hull Cobia runabout that came with the house. Abundantly shaded, with a horseshoe-shaped cove and an undeveloped long view of open water, the place was heaven.

The house itself was small, two bedrooms and one-and-a-half baths. The kitchen was a little rustic, but not terribly. Over the years, the deck got wobbly from holding up our friends and family, so we replaced it. We had someone clean the fallen trees from our woods. We refreshed our gravel drive. Plumbing tended to be a problem even though we drained the pipes before each freeze. A second home is work. There's always something crumbling, rotting, busted, broken.

We didn't cotton much to manicuring. There was no lawn to trim or water, just tall slender South Carolina oaks and pines. On occasion we'd sweep the ever-present lacework of spider webs or scrub the mildew that crept along the outside walls. When the decorative flourishes around the roof rotted we just sawed them off. Every fall we'd spend a glorious day burning leaves, always a meditation practice for me.

We closed on the place two months before learning I was pregnant. We were blessed with both lake property and a beautiful blue-eyed baby, but in the early years, the stress of keeping up with our daughter at the lake was daunting. *Who has Madison? You're in charge of Madison. Don't take your eyes off Madison.* We bought a dozen life preservers, starting with an infant-sized one and progressing to those with straps between the legs for toddlers and on to ones that fit a small woman.

Even though I grew up around water, I never learned to swim properly. I can tread water, probably save myself within a reasonable distance, but those 4-H camp lifesaving lessons were lost on me. If we were to be lake people, I was determined my daughter would be a fish. After swimming lessons

Madison Cotterill with the catch of the day, 2012. Photograph courtesy of the author.

and a few seasons on a swim team, Madison could launch herself from our dock, swim the considerable distance to our neighbor's dock, flip like a dolphin and swim back. Her swimming ability amazed and delighted me.

Still, I made her wear a life vest until she was fifteen. She hated me for it.

When she was young, life preservers were the only way I could relax and enjoy the lake because my daughter had inherited my love of all things creepy-crawly. In our seventeen years at the Lake House, she turned over every log and rock around our cove multiple times. I had two rules. She had to wear shoes and her life vest. Other than that, I didn't care what she did.

When we arrived she would bolt for the shoreline to start poking around. Sometimes she floated along with her goggled face in the water watching fish swim by. I've seen her drift silently until she washed up against a bale of turtles and then snatch one from its sunny spot on a log. She's brought snakes into our house, corralled scorpions and spiders and caught dozens and dozens of fish, sometimes with a pole, but often barehanded.

None of the critter catching bothered me, but to my city-boy husband it was a nightmare. I'd be sunning on the dock, reading in my lounge chair when he'd come down from the house.

"Where's Madison?" he'd ask.

I'd motion across the water and say, "Somewhere over there catching snakes." Even despite his midsummer tan I could detect color draining from his face.

In 2006 an infestation of aquatic weed caused SCE&G to draw down the water. It dropped so low we could walk across our cove to the other bank. During that time we parked our boat on the hillside. The water remained low for much longer than anticipated, and our watercraft rotted.

It was a huge loss to our family fun. I itched to be on the water, wind in my hair, teeth rattling each time we hit a wave. We'd take the Cobia across the big water to a marina that served amazing hamburgers and fries and cold, cold beer. Often we rode up the Saluda River, which feeds Lake Murray, to escape the chop of big water. On the Saluda I would urge Madison to try to ski, but she was more interested in swimming or exploring a new shoreline, so I didn't push her.

I regret that. For me, skiing isn't just an athletic challenge. It's a great metaphor for life—lean into things that scare you, and it doesn't matter if you wipe out. Eventually, you'll pop back to the surface, recover, and get up and give it another go.

I often long for my chair on the deck at the Lake House. I wrote plenty of prose there, coffee in hand, the morning sun like diamonds on the water. And I'll miss our family and friends launching themselves off the high dock to see who could make the biggest splash. We floated until we were waterlogged, our feet touching the cooler water below. We'd get out only to refresh drinks and reapply sunscreen. I'll miss the campfires and roasted marshmallows, chubby sunburned cheeks, and long view of the lake from the hammock.

We sold the Lake House in 2013. It was time. Madison was preparing for college, and the long trek out and the upkeep had become a burden. The new owners are lovely people who live there all year and keep the place up far better than we could from a distance. I'm happy for them to have it. They have grandchildren, and it was with a full heart that I left twelve little life vests hanging neatly in the shed. ↄ

Federal Aid Project #81, Charleston County, Concrete Road, by Melchers, Charleston, S.C. Courtesy of the South Caroliniana Library, University of South Carolina, Columbia, S.C.

Mile Markers

As the road signs say, The End is Near. Something is about to happen.

Dot Jackson, *Refuge* (2006)

)

Almost There

When I was a boy growing up in Greenville, my family used to pile into our car on Sunday afternoons, our father aiming the nearly new '63 Biscayne up U.S. 25, the original two-lane—a winding shady back road that gradually gained altitude, taking us along creeks, past waterfalls, through the Greenville watershed thick with rhododendron and mountain laurel, along the Green River and past the little towns of Tuxedo and Flat Rock. In the summer we rode with the windows down, breathing in the cool, moist air that seemed somehow lighter and richer. I loved that highway for its intimacy, the road curving back on itself, slowing drivers and allowing us time to absorb the ascent up into the mountains—the produce stands, the craft stores, the well-kept little motels, the occasional cabin with smoke curling out of its chimney. We'd sometimes drive as far as Hendersonville, where we'd play miniature golf, then eat fried chicken, green beans, and cornbread at a restaurant whose name escapes me but whose two large black concrete dogs guarding the front entrance I will never forget. Then we'd drive back home feeling like we'd really been somewhere.

That original U.S. 25 shaped me and fed my love for the mountains, and it could be argued that it played a part in me eventually falling in love with and marrying a woman who loved the mountains herself, which is why, after living ten places in our first ten years of marriage, we returned to Asheville in 1989 to raise a family. However, my children would never know the old U.S. 25, at least in the way I had. By the time I'd graduated from Greenville High the old highway was usurped by a gleaming new four-lane, so much sleeker, straighter, and faster. I remember riding along old U.S. 25 somewhere around Tuxedo and suddenly being aware that the light was too bright, then looking up and seeing a huge stripped gouge in the landscape, part of the new highway being built above the old road. I remember the sadness and foreboding that overtook me as I studied the excoriated terrain laid so brutally bare.

Forty-some years later the old U.S. 25 feels more like a childhood dream, my own private tree-lined route, just off everybody's map. The new highway, which is how I still think of it even though it's decades old, is so much quicker and more convenient. And ever since Connie and I moved to Asheville it's kept me connected to my hometown—to my parents, to my friends, and to Greenville itself. At this point, I've probably traveled it more than any other stretch of road in my life.

Although not nearly as cozy and secluded as the old highway, the new highway has its own charms. The old highway, so deep in the woods and sunk into the landscape, was often dark, full of shade and shadow.

The "old" U.S. Highway 25, 1995. Photograph by Steve Marlow.

The "new" U.S. Highway 25, 1975.
Photograph by Steve Marlow.

The new highway, which cuts a wide swath through the mountains, is full of light. In hundreds of trips up and down the new highway, I've witnessed sunrises and sunsets that drenched the mountains in such unearthly pinks and purples I felt I was driving through a Maxfield Parrish painting. The highway is also full of weather. Because the highway traverses the Blue Ridge escarpment it seems to have its own self-contained weather system. Depending on the time of year, you can't be sure if you'll encounter rain, fog, snow, or sleet, and it doesn't seem to be especially related to the weather happening in Asheville or Greenville.

The new U.S. 25 saw me through fatherhood, when we would take our two children down to Greenville to visit my parents. For years it delivered me in a dependable and timely manner to my parents' house so I might help my mother with my ailing father. It ushered me to the nursing home where, against my mother's wishes, we had to put my father his last year. And on a warm clear afternoon in mid-June 2000, I made the drive down the mountain after my brother called to tell me our father had died, and he wouldn't be moved until I could get there. The mountains, the trees, even the drifting clouds seemed in hyper focus, the world shimmering with my father's essence.

After my father's death, the highway kept me connected to my mother during the ten good years she thrived without a sick husband to care for, through the transition time when it became clear she could no longer live at home, through the past year and a half in which she's lived, mostly happily, at an assisted living facility. And this past summer the highway has taken me down to help my brother go through everything in our mother's house, after which I drove an empty Penske rental truck down from Asheville and back up groaning with furniture, books, paintings, and generations of memories.

Still, the highway hasn't been all about endings. It takes me to meet my daughter, a freshman at Furman, the fifth generation of our family to attend, for occasional Friday lunches in Travelers Rest or downtown Greenville. And it generously brings our daughter back to us, when, once in a blue moon, she comes home to do her laundry and visit high school friends who've also come home for the weekend from UNC or NC State. Her mother and I cherish these incidental visits, which would've been more dangerous and taken much longer if the tortuous old U.S. highway were still the only way up the mountain.

In all its constancy, the new highway has witnessed the transitions in my life. And over the years, I've come to appreciate it for itself rather than for where it's getting me. The quiet stretch from Flat Rock, past Tuxedo and then down the mountain into South Carolina and into Travelers Rest has become a kind of respite, a forty-five-minute meditative retreat and even at times a source of solace.

Recently I pieced together a back-road two-lane route from my mother's assisted living facility, through north Greenville neighborhoods, then up through farms and fields, and into the rolling hills of upper Greenville County. It's a relief to drive that slow sweet road after those visits. And the farther I get up the road and the more the mountains and woods close in around me, the more like myself I feel. The passing landscape reminds me that home isn't so much about arriving anywhere as it is going for a ride. ⌒

Ruts

You can get lost there, sometimes stuck, sometimes for years. They don't always show up on maps: dirt roads, years, pickup trucks, and hand-me-down cars wedged along embankments, these paths scraped in the dirt. When you grow up on a dirt road, there is nothing much to do. You walk up and down along the dirt banks with one foot holding you steady at the top while the other falls along the side pushing down as much as your weight can stand. Occasionally you find things—bottles, a confederate belt buckle, jaw bones of fox or wild dog. It's enough to keep you walking, but you can only walk so far before you hate the taste of dust in your mouth. You get older, learn to drive, use the ruts and tracks laid before you as a guide, and it doesn't take long before the banks work as bumpers.

Most of these roads were built in the 1940s, some by the WPA, some by necessity for living. But most were a path to something at some point, connecting fields and logging tracts, perhaps a well-used trail to a springhead or a still. They get the name "dirt road" because they are unpaved, and scrapers provided by the county remove the top layer (generally silica) once a month depending on traffic and weather. Most dirt roads require the scraper to make at least three passes. If you grow up watching *The Dukes of Hazzard*, you learn two things quickly. One is to avoid county scrapers head-on and ride their wake, a foot-and-a-half dirt bank left in the middle of the road. Two, dirt makes you stupid. There are more than seven hundred dirt roads in Lexington County, and you can get fooled quickly into thinking they are all connected. Crout Pond Way has nothing to do with Crout Place; there are two Martin Smith roads—one is a partial runway for crop dusters, and the other goes on forever. You could be on a dirt road for hours, driving 25–30 mph, and think you have gone clear into the other county, only to see that you never left Gilbert. Some dirt roads lead to sand pits.

When you are younger, you play in the sand pits. Not understanding physics as it should have been taught at the time, you may think that sand pits were used to make dirt roads. A mouth open and spitting dirt at the sky. What goes up comes down. What settles through the canopy of scrub oak and sparkleberry is the dirt road, and you are swallowed in it. At night, when the moon is its brightest, the gypsum and silica shimmer, so you move slower and learn to walk with your eyes cut just below the horizon. It numbs you out to the silence of the woods. Might as well be diamonds shimmering, and you might as well have no hands.

When four boys in an '83 Buick Regal each decide to roll a joint, it's not unusual. When they pass around joints behind an abandoned chicken house, it's not unusual. It's not unusual for boys to tell stories about the maiming of men and the girls they wish they could fuck. It's not unusual to hear the rattle of a car on a dirt road before you see the lights. When the sun comes up and someone whispers that it's time to go, it's not unusual to repeat events while creeping towards the truck stop, where it is not unusual to find men with no teeth still drinking coffee, nor is it unusual to find one who'll give you a cigarette. They know where you've been, the dust on your shoulder, it's not unusual.

Take A. C. Bouknight to Camp Branch, Camp Branch to Reedy O. Smith, cut over to Marcelles, and hook back over to Martin Smith, then Goldie to Bouknight to Rimrock, over to Windy Wood, down Elbert Taylor to Sampson, and listen to sides A and B of R.E.M.'s *Reckoning,* the Cramps' *Bad Music for Bad People,* Allman Brothers Band's *Eat a Peach,* and call it Friday night. The next night take Harley Taylor to Craps-Weeks (where truly beautiful people live, seriously, everyone on that road just looks good) to Warner, repeating the trek until the gas is low or you run out of beer, and call it your life before you turn twenty-one.

It won't be long before meth labs move in, and there will be some dirt roads you will never want to go down again. But in between the overlap of pavement and drainage run-off, there are the places where you can stop— a shack called the Shed where Doug teaches you the bass line to a Sex Pistols' song or the pipelines where you build fires, drink from jars, and bleed from your throat. In those places, you forget what brought you there in the first place. The pavement is miles away. There is nothing here that can hurt you.

Nathan Miller Road.
Photograph courtesy of the author.

The local paper says it costs the county roughly $600,000 to pave one mile of dirt road. The decision as to which road gets paved follows a set criteria, but no one outside the county council knows what it is. So it's left to private developers to turn fields into housing developments, and some agree to pave the right-of-way; others pack crush and run. Slowly and at random, these veins are withering. If you live on a dirt road, you welcome this change. If you move away from living on a dirt road, you can't help but feel like an old friend, one who has been with you and there for you when you needed nothing more than to just get away, is going away and never coming back. It's yet another permanent reminder that growing up is just a stroke of luck.

You would be within your rights to think that nothing good happens on dirt roads, to pave them all, but good has nothing to do with it. A kid once smashed a girl's head in on the railroad tracks, another dropped a concrete block off a bridge killing a baby on the interstate, and in 1989 someone dumped a body across the street from Gilbert Elementary School—not on dirt roads.

There are rivers that run through some counties. Railroads too. But dirt roads do not run through anything. They wrap around like a vine or virus. If you grow up around them, they become a part of you, and sooner or later you will become a part of them. Run over the same tract of skin with your fingernail until you reach bone. Poke a hole in your eye and look through the runoff. Hold a rusty soup can to the sun just before you eat it. That is what it is like to be a dirt road. After a hard rain, you can see where a dirt road held the washout before it drowned. In the summer, it draws into itself and scatters in the dust. It waits there faithfully.

Go to the dirt road drunk or sober. Put your face to it and hear what it has to say before you start talking. Know your place. And when it's your turn to talk, talk slow. ☽

Valerie Sayers

Looking for the Light

If we wanted to look for the light, we went as a couple on an excuse for a date, or we went as Marines with six-packs of beer, or we went as giggly gaggles of girls. On Friday nights when there was no football game, no dance, no action, we lined the shoulders of the Land's End Road on St. Helena Island, white kids in the middle of a rich Gullah culture. We were oblivious. We huddled in cars under live oaks dangling clumps of moss as luxuriant as a biblical patriarch's beard. In the dark lowcountry night, we smooched or drank ourselves silly or both, the Beach Boys seeping out of car radios while we waited for the light.

The light was a ball of fire, or it was a glow—a white glow, a green glow, an uncanny vaporous glow—and it came down the middle of the road straight toward your car, or it whooshed up from the ditch, or it floated through the trees. You saw it out at Fort Fremont, or under the biggest oak, or just past the crossroad. You had to sit stone-still, respectful, or you had to get out of your car and summon it with the loudest, meanest cusses you knew. You had to spit on graves, and you had to fall on your knees. It was swamp gas, our parents said, but we knew better. It was a ghost, and all the competing versions of what it looked like didn't make it one jot less real. We knew scores of kids who'd seen it.

To inoculate ourselves against our next nighttime visit, we drove the Land's End Road in daytime, too. We came from Beaufort and headed out on the beach road until the turn at the Corner Co-operative in Frogmore. Most of us had no idea that Frogmore was the name of a plantation, or that in a few years that name would be contested by folks who were sick of hearing about plantations. We drove past what was left of the Chapel of Ease,

Land's End Road.
Photograph by John Shurr.

where eighteenth-century planters who couldn't make it into town came for Sunday services. Some said you could see the light right there, among the crumbling tombstones, if you waited long enough. If we'd known anything, we might have looked at the elegant ruins and imagined the slaves sitting separately in the chapel, but we were ignorant yahoos. We didn't even know about the other houses of worship all around us: the praise houses on St. Helena built by the slaves, and later the freed slaves, to keep an old faith alive with a new one.

Past the Chapel of Ease we passed field upon lush field where rice once flourished, where row upon row once yielded cotton, where in our day Mexican migrant workers picked tomatoes and cucumbers in back-twisting labor. Did we contemplate the slaves who once worked those fields? Black churches and gravestones dotted the sides of the road: sometimes it seemed they popped up every time the odometer registered another tenth of a mile. We might have heard rumors that Dr. Martin Luther King came down to the Penn Center. We might even have had vague notions about the Yankee do-gooders who had come down here to teach the freed slaves. But few of us had any sense of the proud history of land ownership and self-sufficiency among the descendants of slaves on St. Helena. We neglected to puzzle why there was a co-op on that corner where we'd turned.

The road ran on for eight miles, the massive old trees reaching toward each other in arches for us to pass through. We headed toward the end of the world, toward dazzling stretches of water where the Beaufort and Broad Rivers would meet in the Port Royal Sound. Just before the end of the land, we turned into Fort Fremont, where, according to eyewitnesses, the light had made many appearances. We—dolts! knuckleheads!—thought it was a fort from the Civil War, but it was built three decades after, during the Spanish-American War, as a lookout. We were at a spot where the wealthy planters of St. Helena had also looked out across the water, to watch the Battle of Hilton Head in 1861. They fled the island and their plantations when they saw that the Confederate cannons couldn't touch the Union gunboats. The slaves who refused to accompany them on their flight from St. Helena and Lady's Island and Beaufort started new lives as free agents months before Emancipation Day the next year.

We didn't know much, we white kids in those early days of integration. We knew the world was turning in a new direction, and some of us embraced the change and some of us fought it with as much bitterness as we could summon. It never occurred to most of us that the African Americans

St. Helena Parish Chapel of Ease.
Photograph by John Shurr.

of St. Helena would have a very different version of the light, that these rich planting fields held a history beyond our fathoming.

But maybe somewhere deep in our collective white unconscious we were imagining the relentless reality of captivity. If some versions of the light made the ghost a plantation owner's child, gone to an early grave like those graves at the Chapel of Ease, others made the light a slave-ghost, coming back to avenge himself for a hanging. What did we white kids know of lashings or beatings or rape? We knew only that the landscape here was powerful in its beauty and its mystery: we still had to learn our terrible shared history.

When I drive out on Land's End these days, I turn at the Red Piano Too, a joyful gallery filled with Gullah art on the site of the old co-op. The road sign at the top of the Land's End Road now says DR. MARTIN LUTHER KING, JR. DRIVE, and the Penn Center that once welcomed Dr. King now welcomes me. Trees and fields, stone and wood stretch out in brilliant balance. I'm filled with the comfort of a return home to the lowcountry. Air and water dance, daylight shimmies, possibilities spark.

People still drive the Land's End Road looking for the light, and people still see it. I'm pretty sure it's a different light now—now the ghost has died in a car crash or a hurricane. Back then we didn't think of accidents, of swollen marshes, of floods. Back then, in the 1960s, a history we didn't know yet hovered in the dark night, waiting for us to learn it: a biblical ball of glowing phosphorescence. We knew our scripture. It was going to be the fire next time. It was going to be the light. ☽

Newberry College Cheerleaders, 1948. Photograph courtesy of Newberry College

Getting into the Game

Looking at it now, you might say Newberry College had a pretty sorry football team in 1948. Underdogs throughout the season, the Indians won two games, lost seven, and didn't score at all for four. Still, the cheerleaders cheered, the fans yelled, and the 1949 *Newberrian* pointed out the positive: Hank Witt's total passing yardage was 927, one of the highest in the country, and Newberry toppled favored Erskine 14–0.

> Commented the *Newberrian*: "The Indians really upset the dope bucket in this one."

)

Capital City Stadium and the Writing Life

Capital City Stadium in the summer of 1999 was a dump through sins of omission, commission, and outright design.

So was my career.

At least the stadium had an excuse. Built in 1927, "the Cap" looked like it'd had about two splashes of paint and an ADA-mandated wheelchair ramp added in the seventy years since. It seemed that as America stopped caring about baseball from the 1950s to 2000, Columbia stopped caring about the stadium. Making matters worse was that the out-of-state own-ership group was trying to muscle the city into building the team a new downtown ballpark and so put off making needed improvements while complaining loudly about the laundry list of issues they let accumulate.

I had no such justification for my own pitiable condition other than an affinity for academia and an aversion to the workplace. A poetry graduate student under James Dickey, I'd let school slide after his death in 1997. In the two years following I squeaked by as a private tutor helping rich kids get good grades and as a tech school writing center adjunct helping adult learners write resumes. When I took a job as a copy editor for the *Dictionary of Literary Biography*, I felt lucky to have a full-time job in the field—until I got my first paycheck.

Grossing $14,000 a year editing "Literature of the French and Occitan Middle Ages" and "Pre-Nineteenth Century British Book Collectors and Bibliographers" forced me to take a second full-time job. For two weeks, from ten at night to seven in the morning, I stocked shelves at Food Lion.

Capital City Stadium. Courtesy of Blowfish Baseball.

After a particularly vivid hallucinatory experience driving on the interstate between jobs, I knew something had to change.

I answered an ad for a part-time "agate clerk" at the *State*. I didn't know what that was, only that the hours worked with my schedule. I quickly learned "agate" refers to the 5.5-point type used for sports statistics, and why the position, internally, was called the "agate maggot." The chief responsibilities were typing high school scores, posting betting lines, and updating the pro standings and scores as they trickled in from the West Coast. It wasn't as dry as chronicling old British book nerds, but it was still dull work.

So offered the chance to get away and see what writers do—oh, how I laughed that they thought themselves "writers"—I saw no reason not to accept. I got in my 1984 Saab and sputtered to the stadium. My assignment was to shadow a freelancer named Jeff for a doubleheader.

It was the first time I'd been to a press box as a member of the working media. Jeff was nowhere, but that was no big deal. I was early. I took out the scorebook I'd just bought and settled into carefully filling out my lineups and taking in the scenery from a perspective I'd never enjoyed.

The game against the Charleston RiverDogs began without Jeff. I'd called his cell phone but got nothing. The first inning went by, then the second, and a creeping worry began. I knew since this story was going in the next day's paper he conceivably could write a recap from the box score alone and no one would care, but still. I phoned the paper, but the seasoned souls on the copy desk did not share my concern about a six-inch story for the Tuesday paper scheduled to run on C6. I soldiered on.

Adding to my growing nervousness was that Charleston's pitcher, Jason Standridge, had a little thing called a no-hitter going. If you've played base-ball, watched baseball, or have ever heard of baseball, you know that during a no-hitter, you do not talk about a no-hitter. You may think about it, but that's it. You try not even to do that, so sacred is the feat.

Yet there it was, a no-hitter through four. Through five. Through six. Through seven—which is when you really start to think about it. And there I was, my collar tightening with every 1-2-3 inning, every smoothly retired side—where the hell is Jeff!!??!!! What in the world do they expect me to do?

They expected me to write a story, I learned when I called for prob-ably the fifth time. I took my notebook, trudged down to the dugout and walked on the field after the final out as if I knew what I was doing. Which I certainly did not.

There was Standridge, the thirty-first overall pick of the 1997 draft by the Tampa Bay Devil Rays, standing six foot three and having just thrown the best game of his life. And there was I, the person responsible for recording it, who had never conducted an interview or taken a journalism class or felt even the modest pride of a high school byline.

I took a deep breath, walked up, and said something clever like "Pretty good game, eh?" I was hoping, praying, he'd say something. My prayers were answered, just not how I expected.

For the next five minutes Standridge told me of his journey with the Lord, how it began, and where it had led him. He told me how on fire he was with the Holy Spirit during the game, how he felt the presence of his Lord and Savior Jesus Christ calming him while on the mound, and did I have a relationship with him?

I listened, befuddled. Was this normal? I tried to write everything down but eventually gave up. Finally I asked him what pitches worked for him, and he gave me some quotes I could use. Relieved, I thanked him, then felt that peculiar atmospheric pressure known to journalists on deadline as I realized I now had to write a story about the game for the largest newspaper in South Carolina.

Taking another deep breath, I drew on what experience I had—teaching English 101 to college freshmen and writing countless papers myself. The classic college paper, I told my students, is a five-paragraph essay with an introduction, three body paragraphs, and a conclusion.

I applied the same formula, and even found enough confidence to get a little flowery with my lede—newspaper-speak for that critical first sentence. Using the threatening pregame weather as a literary device, I wrote something like this: "Rain clouds loomed large over Capital City Stadium Monday; Charleston RiverDogs pitcher Jason Standridge, however, loomed larger."

As ledes go, it was a foul thing, the product of an academic background that also influenced my byline choice. Rather than "Ron Aiken," the name I answer to, I wrote "Ronald D. Aiken II" because as everyone knows in academia, the longer your name, the more impressive you seem. I even dallied with spelling out my middle name. Besides providing comedy for the copy desk, I was razzed mercilessly by the other writers. In some circles, I'll always be "Deuce."

Despite the lede, the story was good enough that I was asked to do it again, though in a final twist it was spiked. Jeff had made it to the park in time for the second game of the doubleheader—he'd had an exam earlier in the day, it turned out—and due to last-minute space constraints the paper ran his single recap of both games.

Still, the fire was lit, and the rest of that summer I probably covered twenty or more games, learning how to report, how to interview, how to describe, how to write—in short, how to be a journalist. I also came to appreciate sports writing, the challenge of a game story, and the comforting rituals of a beat against which splash those rare moments of triumph, like the one that launched my career.

Summer turned to fall, baseball into football, football into basketball, and the freelance work into a full-time position as a staff writer at the *State*. Less than a year after that no-hitter, I had a job and career unimaginable to me a year before when I was stocking shelves at midnight hoping no one I knew saw me and slaving over "Dutch Dandies of the Middle Ages" (okay, I made that one up) while agonizing over whether to go back and finish my M.F.A. in poetry or stay at the publishing company with the hope of one day making editor and buying a car made in the last ten years.

Sixteen summers and a fruitful career later, I drive by Capital City Stadium and don't even look. It's like driving by your old high school: it's barely changed, you're barely the same. The memories remain, however, of that summer at the Cap where I learned how to write and where a career I never intended nor had any ambition toward so auspiciously began.

Writer's note: Jason Standridge compiled a career 3–9 record in the Major Leagues from 2001 to 2007 and pitches for the Fukuoka SoftBank Hawks of the Japanese Professional League. Capital City Stadium's career has been equally uneven and ultimately tragic. It lost minor league baseball for good when the team moved to Greenville, South Carolina, in 2005 and squeaked by hosting the Columbia Blowfish of the Coastal Plain League, the Benedict College Tigers, and various exhibition games until 2014, when the last baseball game was played between the Blowfish and the Thomasville (North Carolina) HiToms on July 31. The property, in use as a baseball stadium since 1927, was bought by an Atlanta-based developer and is slated for demolition to make way for a mixed-use retail location anchored by a Kroger grocery store. ☽

The Passion of Eighty
Thousand in One

Since moving to South Carolina in 1998, I've found myself drawn to many places that are warm, comfortable, serene, and beautiful. Our first home in a quiet Columbia neighborhood had a large private swimming pool, something my New England self had wanted forever. It provided intermittent refuge from the heavy task of unpacking eighteen years of a life we'd left behind. That decision was right whenever I floated cool and weightless there, staring up at a blue sky, surrounded by enormous perennial hibiscus. I lived in the pool spring, summer, and fall. Still, the most luscious memories are of 10 P.M. dips midsummer, when the water was finally a few degrees cooler than the air.

When our younger child left home at sixteen to study and reside at the South Carolina Governor's School for the Arts and Humanities in Greenville, that home echoed in the silent void of my barely beating heart. It was the definition of sad, as if a cloud were fixed over the pool, darkening the water. My husband had the idea that surviving the empty nest meant we didn't stay there either—brilliant! So we started exploring South Carolina on the weekends.

We picked a Victorian B&B in Georgetown one weekend and enjoyed the broad main street with a tiny garden shop, floors of antiques, delicious food. Sunday morning came, and in chatting with the other guests, we were directed to Brookgreen Gardens. It was by far the most beautiful place in South Carolina. I immediately envisioned our daughter's wedding in the majestic oak allée. Anna Hyatt Huntington's sculptures, accented by her husband Archer's poems, anchored bright, formal gardens.

Slender-stemmed poppies in soft yellows, pinks, and melons blushed in the slightest breeze, slowing my breath. For me, it was a spiritual world.

Brookgreen was the best place in South Carolina until 2008, when we moved into the President's House on the Historic Horseshoe at the University of South Carolina. The house, used as a public space as many as two hundred times every academic year, doubles as a haven from the public life we lead. When we enter our apartment overlooking the garden on the back, we unwind like all couples—we prop slippered feet on ottomans, read through stacks of mail or good books, or absently flip channels.

We love looking out the large windows onto the Horseshoe at the passersby—students, faculty, staff, alumni, and neighbors with babies and dogs. We have our own mini city right at our front door. Sometimes students ring the bell looking for a photo op, sometimes just to say hello, and sometimes bearing cookies. We consider ourselves blessed to rest our heads at night in the warmth of the USC community.

And while I may not have my swimming pool in the back yard, I do have a smaller version of Brookgreen. It's beautiful, colorful, and fragrant, but it also provides a refuge for all kinds of birds, the Horseshoe's abundant squirrel population, and me. On the days when it's not being dressed up for an event, the President's House garden is a quiet retreat.

I have written about the garden, because it is truly my heart's first go-to place. So why am I writing now about Williams-Brice Stadium? In a word, Penelope.

Penelope is our first grandchild. She lives with our daughter and son-in-love (a term I adopted from my own mother-in-love), and baby sister Alice Anastasia in Santa Monica—yes, sadly, California. In their home, the Lakers hold the only athletic interest—at least, until their visit east. I've been to Williams-Brice for sixteen football seasons, melting through countless baking hot afternoons in the west-facing stands. But for the last seven seasons I've watched from the President's box, climate-controlled with cushioned seats.

I relish having some input into the SEC football experience in this box, especially choosing the menus. Our guests are polite, and if they miss the hotdogs too desperately, they know where to go at halftime to grab one. I've created an atmosphere in our little space where I could learn to love football and I have.

That being said, the box is not calm like the garden. We've experienced frequent episodes of high blood pressure and stress headaches, not to mention outbursts. Watching Marcus Lattimore get hurt for the second time

Penelope Erickson surveys the scene at Williams-Brice Stadium.
Photograph courtesy of Katharine Erickson.

broke our hearts, until his beautiful example of resilience prevailed. But when Penelope at nineteen months attended her first game there, on my lap, I saw the beauty of Williams-Brice in a new way. New eyes propelled it to the very top of the list of places in my heart.

It was the Clemson game, November 30, 2013. Penelope had danced around the tailgate, pulled grass, chased cousins, met donors, and shyly curled into her dad's shoulder when Cocky approached. But when we finally made it to the box, she was mellow, pacifier in mouth. We expected her to fall asleep.

She settled into my lap, but not in the posture of sleep. Her back was erect as she absorbed the scene that is USC football. She clapped with the band and cheered with the fans. Then "Sandstorm" started. Within its first three beats, this pulsating techno song had eighty thousand Gamecock fans jumping up and down in the stands, wildly waving rally towels and shouting "USC! USC!" Penelope waved her rally towel with the best of them—this I have on tape! She did what her papou advises all our students: "Participate!" Wow, did she participate!

Just when the guests in the President's box were electrified by her energy, and all eyes were on her, our dear Penelope pulled the pacifier from her mouth and shouted "Go Cocks!" She then calmly reinserted the "soothie," pointed to her sweater, which bore the great block C, then pointed to her cousin Mackenzie's Gamecock necklace.

Within the span of fifteen minutes, Penelope had connected the band, Cocky, the team, the cheering crowd, "Sandstorm," the block C, *and* felt the excitement that is Gamecock football.

She didn't last the whole game, and she's yet to fathom the significance of the rivalry, or what it means to our fans to have defeated Clemson five consecutive years. But our sweet Penelope felt the sheer visceral energy reverberating through Williams-Brice Stadium, an energy she leapt into with all she had, an energy that brought us victory *again!*

The spirit of Williams-Brice is alive in the off-season during our Face-Time chats with California. They now end like most of Papou's speeches, with a "One, two, three: Go Gamecocks!" ☽

Caesar's Head. Courtesy of the South Caroliniana Library,
University of South Carolina, Columbia, S.C.

Communing

My Grandmother Bowen, when she wished to be alone, would walk to
the tops of mountains and stare into immeasurable space; my Great-Aunt
Narcissa would slip under dark rhododendron bushes and sit by the deep
pools in the dimness of half-light and silence. I think my Great-Aunt
Narcissa suspected that life came out of darkness, that the spirit welled
from the depths.

Ben Robertson, (1903–1943), *Red Hills and Cotton: An Upcountry Memory.*

⏝

Pond Watcher

Once I lived in an Airstream trailer, located in the midst of a Saluda County forest of pines and scattered hardwoods. My companions in solitude were three cats and two dogs. I was supposed to keep the animals domesticated; they made me a little wild.

One dog was a blonde Labrador; the other was a small bundle of long hair, an elongated body, and enormous bug eyes. The cats curled next to me on the bed at night, lulling me to sleep with their purring. This display of domesticity was deceptive; they arose in the night to hunt. I'd awake to golden eyes shining like witch fire as the cats watched me before stalking out into the darkness on their nocturnal prowls. Both cats and dogs came and went as they pleased through the pet access door. The dogs loyally remained. For the first few days both dogs stayed underfoot until the two trusted me not to disappear. Although they had twenty-seven acres to roam, they wanted a routine. We walked in the morning before the sun rose and in the evenings before the sun set. We explored old logging roads cut through the pines and the abandoned paths of deer hunters. As winter days shortened, we sometimes walked at night. On nights of the full moon, the illumination was so bright the trees cast shadows, and the banshee wails of coyotes rent the air.

A pond lay at the heart of the property. Its shape reminded me of a rough triangle, with the dam as the base and the point disappearing into the woods. Paths on either side led to the trailer door. Since the pond was a few feet from the trailer door, it became the starting point for all our journeys.

The kitchen windows faced the pond. I used the table as a desk for my research and writing but spent most of my time watching the wild fowl on the water, binoculars and *Birds of the Carolinas* close at hand. Hawks rode the wind currents, blue herons picked through the shallows, and once a turkey hen strutted into the clearing. Wild ducks circled the pond in a slowly descending pattern, wings and tails outspread to slow their speed as they lowered their feet and glided onto the surface of the water. The larger male ducks had glossy, green heads, brown breast feathers, and glints of purple and gray brown on the wings and back. Smaller females weren't as brightly colored, with feathers in hues of brown, black, and gray. I watched the ducks paddle over the pond, tipping their heads down into the water as they fed, feet and tail feathers waving in the air. In the spring scarlet drops of blood splashed over the ground as the cardinals returned. After feeding, the cardinals flew into the oak trees, vivid red blurs against the bare gray branches. The sight of the first hummingbird sipping from the feeder marked the true return of spring.

I told concerned friends the dogs were protection against intruders. In truth the two snarled at innocent water fowl and greeted my few human visitors with wagging tails. I suspect they might have fawned on Jack the Ripper. One of the cats presented me with a bird. I snatched it, cradling the small brown body carefully until I felt the tiny heart beat against my palms, and released it into the frozen night. The cat sulked for days, venting its fury on the mouse foolish enough to invade the bedroom.

One morning before the first frost I encountered a large, brown dog curled up on the dam, basking in the sunshine. The dogs didn't bark. Perhaps this was a frequent and familiar visitor. The dog raised its head and slowly uncurled. The paddle tail waved in the air and thumped down on the dam's surface. I had never before seen a beaver in its natural habitat. The animal regarded us curiously, unalarmed at our approach. The beaver was larger than the dogs, and I must not have appeared threatening. The animal scrutinized us for a few minutes, slowly got to its feet, and waddled to the edge of the pond. It slipped effortlessly into the water and slid beneath the surface.

From the stone bench I watched the pond's still waters. The dogs moved on, bored with my inactivity. After a few minutes, a sleek brown head broke the surface of the pond. The beaver paddled a few strokes before it dove back down into the dark depths. *Ker-lumph!* The broad tail smacked against the surface.

Beavers don't always build lodges, I learned later. They sometimes create dens by burrowing into the banks of ponds or streams. After the first sighting, I frequently sat by the edge of the pond, hoping for a glimpse of the beaver. I always thought of it as "he." Sometimes he rewarded my patience.

He'd surface and swim in lazy circles, his slow strokes drawing him nearer to the water's edge. He turned his head to stare at me with dark eyes. I held my breath. On his last circular passage he stopped, treading water as he regarded me as intensely as I stared at him. With a shudder he ducked his nose under the silent waters and dove, signaling his descent with a large thwack of his tail.

The full moon in winter is known as a diamond ice moon, from the halo circling it as the moisture in the air freezes into ice crystals. The frost-covered ground glistened in the moonlight and crunched under my feet as I walked. The cold seeped into my bones. Back inside, gloves off, I found the tips of my fingers white from the cold. I had to rub my hands vigorously before the blood circulated in my fingers once again.

The next morning light rain drizzled from a milky sky. Droplets pelted on the wide-brimmed hat I wore and turned the surface of the pond into overlapping circles. By midmorning the temperature dropped and the rain froze before it hit the ground. Bare tree branches blossomed with crystal ice flowers and the sleet-covered ground glittered in the pale light. By midaft-ernoon, the landscape had become an ice garden. Showing no inclination to go outside, the dogs sprawled contentedly on the floor.

In the small hours of the night, loud cracking noises jolted me into wakefulness. Frozen trees and limbs were breaking around me. In my groggy state, I'd thought it was rifle fire. Finally I became so accustomed to the sound I fell asleep again.

After a few hours I woke in gray light. The cold, not the light, awakened me. We lost electrical power for five days.

Walking briskly in the sunlight kept me warmer than huddling inside. I pulled a knit cap over my ears, zipped up my insulated jacket, and thrust my hands into heavy gloves. I marveled at the glittering diamond-spangled tree branches and crunching frozen grasses. A few large limbs littered the way to the pond. Most of the breakage had occurred among the pines. The chill air smelled of sweet resin.

Ker-lumph! The sound came from my left. Another tree limb must have cracked under the strain of the freeze. *Ker-lumph!* The plop echoed over the pond's surface. The dogs pawed gingerly at the thin shell of ice on the edges of the pond. A sleek dark head glided through the deeper unfrozen waters.

The beaver slowly swam in a large circle, swimming nearer and nearer to the bank where I stood. The two dogs silently watched. I could have reached out and touched him as he swam by. He paused, regarding me with liquid eyes. He dove beneath the waters, his broad tail smacking the surface before he disappeared.

As the days grew warmer, I spent more time sitting near the pond. I watched the wind ripple across the surface and splinter the water into patterns of dancing light. The Celts viewed bodies of water as the gateways between two worlds, the world of the everyday and a magical world beneath the waters. Medieval mystics practiced scrying, gazing into a bowl of water until they saw visions. I began to think if I gazed at the waters of the pond long and hard enough, I, too, would see visions.

I kept a journal of my solitude and discovered fulfillment in spinning the gold of memory into the straw of words. From the journal I progressed to other forms of writing—short stories, novels, travel articles. Life between the water and the woods suited me. When I returned to the life in a town, I found life too fast, too loud. In English legends mortals seduced into entering the secret realm of the elves regretted their stay when they returned to the world of mankind. My time in the woods near the pond, with dogs, cats, and a beaver for companions, was a time spent in a secret world. I didn't regret the stay; I regretted the return.

There are moments in life when we realize we'll compare the rest of our days to the time when we forever change. Some mornings in that Saluda County forest, thick mists rose from the pond like dragon's breath, swirled across the waters, and drifted toward the trailer. The swirling mists gave me the impression that spirits from the world beneath the waters had pierced the veil and entered this world. I recalled the words of Genesis. "And the Spirit of God moved upon the face of the waters." As I watched by the pond in the woods, I learned the meaning of those words. ꙃ

Ronald Daise

Ancient Voices Beckoning, Pleading

The Lowcountry Trail at Brookgreen Gardens had been calling out to me before I saw it or began working here in 2004. The country's premier sculpture garden, established on four former rice plantations in 1931, is renowned for its stunning display of art and pristine beauty. By hearing and answering the call of ancestral voices along this winding, paved quarter-mile path, I've influenced a dimension of our historic interpretation. In so doing, my love for this place has deepened.

My office overlooks the beginning of the Lowcountry Trail. Daily I view a hand-dug canal leading to freshwater creeks and tidal inlets and also Mainfield, the main rice field, among several others, on which about five hundred enslaved Africans on Brookgreen Plantation once worked. It is one of my favorite sites because my contemplations as I look out of my window are of home, heritage, and history.

Aged and spectacular live oaks, beautified with Spanish moss, bring an almost palpable mystery to the trail. Their presence inspires childhood memories of magnificent live oak trees on the grounds of Penn Center on St. Helena Island, South Carolina, my homeland. I would climb and sit atop low-hanging, outstretched limbs that bowed to the ground then curled back upward. "These limbs are strong limbs!" I remember thinking. Those limbs witnessed my parents attending classes at the Penn School, the first southern school for freed enslaved Africans, and their graduating in the class of 1933. Those limbs swayed with majesty to jubilant and plaintive songs sung at the Community Sing programs in the Frissell Community House I attended throughout childhood. And those limbs saw the pain and cruelty inflicted upon others during the period of slavery, the incendiary crosses burned by Klansmen on the campus in the not-too-distant past, and the pride of many who heard the Reverend Dr. Martin Luther King Jr., Alex Haley, and Sierra Leonean president Joseph Momoh speak on these grounds.

Those low-hanging limbs, cut down in the 1970s, stir my imagination now as I walk the Lowcountry Trail. I wonder what stories the oaks here can tell of celebration, pain and suffering, sorrow, joy.

I've traveled throughout coastal communities of the federal Gullah Geechee Cultural Heritage Corridor, from Wilmington, North Carolina, to St. Augustine, Florida. Some subdivisions, communities, and historic sites are built atop grounds where my Gullah Geechee ancestors once lived and labored. In those sites where I've immediately sensed "dis-spiritedness," I've quickly retreated and rarely returned. I accept that others may not understand or acknowledge what to me is real, but I've learned to obey a directive in a spiritual I learned as a child, *"You betta go when the spirit say, 'Go!'"* Then again a line from another spiritual comes to me along the Lowcountry Trail: *"We been comin a long time. Oh, yes!"* I feel at peace along the trail. It is imbued with respectfulness of heritage.

Viewers see depictions of historic sites that were unearthed during an archeological dig in the 1990s. The footprints of the overseer's kitchen, the smokehouse, and the slave dependency (a cabin of the overseer's cook) dot the landscape, along with four unique sculptures of characters who shaped Gullah Geechee culture. Unlike other sculptures at Brookgreen Gardens, *The Planter, The Overseer, The Enslaved African Female,* and *The Enslaved African Male* are constructed of stainless steel and cut with laser beams. "These sculptures were placed here so that we could understand our past and embrace our future," sculptor Babette Bloch said when her work was unveiled in 2006. "They are portals of times gone by, mirrors to our souls. I believe these sculptures will evoke a range of emotions, from pride of place to mourning. They are echoes of the lives that lived on this historic site. When the sun is behind the figures, they will read as silhouettes. And when the sun dances over the surfaces, the figures are a shimmering silver, imbued and filled with the hues of the surrounding landscape."

Sometimes the sculptures catch me unawares and stand apparition-like. Because nature is viewed through them, they seem to move. Reality eerily becomes blurred.

My travels to Ghana in 2004 and Sierra Leone in 2005 afforded me opportunities to see firsthand connections with West African and Gullah Geechee cultures. The trips were fortuitous to my sharing with visitors at Brookgreen Gardens the history of Gullah Geechee people, particularly

The Enslaved African Male by sculptor Babette Bloch.
Photograph courtesy of Brookgreen Gardens.

descendants of West African rice growers who were brought to Georgetown for the production of rice. Their technological skill, knowledge, and labor on the approximately forty-five thousand rice fields along the Waccamaw Neck produced more than half of this country's wealth in the 1700s and shaped the American cultural fabric.

When I walked the site of what would become the Lowcountry Trail upon my arrival at Brookgreen Gardens, I sensed the presence of ancestral spirits. I heard their voices whispering, "Tell de wol bout we. Tell dem bout all we done done. All we come shru. You yeddy me?" Today, as I venture along in one of my favorite places, I am confident the ancestral spirits keeping watch are pleased. ☽

))

Quietly, by a Crashing Cascade

I was eighteen when I stood atop a spectacular waterfall on the edge of South Carolina, watching a crystal river plunge down a cliff and tumble toward a deep lake that sparkled in the distance. It was late on a July afternoon, the sun dropping and the twilight gathering as I positioned myself on a flat rock near the lip of the falls. I could see for miles across the hazy blue mountains and into the South Carolina foothills.

The lake rippled gently, filling the coves around verdant peninsulas of hemlocks and hardwoods. The summer sounds of tree frogs and crickets lifted out of the nearby forest as the river rushed past me and toward the falls. Peaceful it was, and I was delighted to have found it. How, I asked, could I have missed this place after all these years?

I had been to the Carolina mountains many times with my family as a young boy, often to visit my great-grandmother. I remember staying at her home, impressed with the beautiful scenery but also the simple life she led. On our trips from Anderson to Franklin, North Carolina, we bunked in her wooden house on a sloping mountainside. MaMa Rouda baked biscuits and cooked spiced apples on a wood stove that made everything extra tasty. We ate sweet muscadines that grew on a vine in her yard and drank near-freezing water, drawn by hand from an open well. I would sometimes climb to the loft of an old barn, filled with hay for the livestock she once kept on the property.

The porch just off her kitchen had a view of the mountains that's embedded in my mind. The hills of North Carolina rose high behind a wide cornfield across a dirt-and-gravel road, creating an almost reverence in me that was reserved for church. The Blue Ridge seemed to last forever.

Lake Jocassee in South Carolina from Whitewater Falls in North Carolina.
Photograph by Jamie Francis, courtesy of *The State* newspaper.

But as I stood at the waterfall that muggy evening years later, gazing into South Carolina's lush mountains, I felt a different respect.

The place was Upper Whitewater Falls in North Carolina, above a river gorge to Lake Jocassee. There aren't many views that compare to this one. To me seeing the lake and South Carolina from another state was a localized version of what the astronauts saw when they viewed the earth from the moon. You were looking at your own domain from another place and realizing how much there was to appreciate.

I could barely make out a forested hillside with a smattering of homes nestled in the trees, and a taller mountain behind it with a ragged top like a rooster's comb. Not far away the lake curved out of sight and toward the Jocassee dam, built to hold back the rivers that flow from western North Carolina into South Carolina.

Say what you'd like about the wisdom of flooding a mountain river valley to create a lake—and there are plenty of arguments against it—Lake Jocassee is a beautiful sight. In all my years of writing about the natural world, no other place makes me feel the way I do when looking toward Jocassee from Upper Whitewater Falls.

It had taken effort to find this place that day in 1979. A winding road in South Carolina led a friend and me past Oconee State Park and through the Sumter National Forest to North Carolina. His small Toyota sputtered along the state line as we searched for a place to camp. We soon crossed a bridge in North Carolina, just over the South Carolina border. Below the span the churning Whitewater River invited us to stop.

Parking the car along the roadside, we took a steep path through the forest next to the bridge and toward the big stream. The sound of rushing water increased as we moved farther down the trail. At an opening in the woods, we could see the gray-green river and its rocky, whitewater shoals. After picking a spot to camp and gulping a quick meal of beans and potatoes, we began to explore.

We hopped across some flat rocks and waded through the water downstream. Ten minutes later, soaked from the river trek, we came upon the view that's impossible to forget. "I've got to come back," I thought to myself as I stared at South Carolina's Lake Jocassee from Upper Whitewater Falls.

Every few years since then, I've visited the upper falls and looked into South Carolina. Sometimes I've been there only a few minutes. Other times it has been longer. Each time I've stood quietly on a boulder by the crashing cascade. The scene has always given me a certain kind of peace.

And every time I've returned, I've brought someone with me. The first was my fiancée, who waded with me through the cold river to the top of the falls and gasped at the steepness of the drop. Another time I took a photojournalist so he could snap pictures during a colorful fall sunrise to illustrate a story I was writing. One of those photos appeared in the *State* newspaper and today, thanks to the girl I married, hangs in a frame on a wall at my house.

Most recently I stopped with my teenage sons as we drove to an uncle's home for a visit. The boys stood on the same rock by the falls and looked into South Carolina, just as I had done when I was their age. I was proud to show them this special place.

I think they liked it. Maybe one day they too will return—only this time, on their own. ༣

☽

Present in the Forest

Paths converge all over Harbison State Forest in Columbia. Those trails followed by hikers in camo and khaki converge with those explored by bikers in helmets and Spandex, only to diverge again, winding their way over twenty-one miles of forested pathways, a short distance from the Broad River.

For me, a different kind of convergence happens when I enter the forest, which depending on the time of year and the hour of the day could be shrouded in mist or mosquitoes. A morning on the Spider Woman, Lost Creek, or Midlands Mountain Trail tests my endurance and connects me with my fifty-year-old core but also helps me disconnect for a few hours from overstimulation, putting nature's calm in place of the barrage of call and response that passes for communication these days.

I began hiking about five years ago as a way to restore the health that thirty years of smoking had depleted and drop a couple of inches off my waist, weight I had put on after I quit and rediscovered the taste of food. I had not anticipated that as the pounds fell off along the trails, I would leave worry and dissatisfaction draped across the branches of the scrub oaks and longleaf pines as well.

When done properly, negotiating the rocky rises and pitches of Spider Woman or the twisting double-backs on Lost Creek or the curving ascents of Midland Mountain will strip away pounds, tone muscles, sharpen agility, and hone coordination. But I also found the trails helped me transcend the physical to reach the spiritual—not the divine, necessarily, but the intangible that is revealed in the elegant coarseness of nature.

The Buddha said, "The foot feels the foot when it feels the ground." That suggests to me the importance of being present for all that I do. I feel the

Bridge to the Midlands Mountain Trail in Harbison State Forest.
Photograph courtesy of the author.

poke of the stone on the sole of my foot, the scratch of the branch on my arm, the tacky tangle of barely-there webs on my face, the sweat pouring down my back, the faint pulsation in my hands. They keep me present. I'm not thinking of where I was before or where I will be in an hour. The nattering worries of a testy and intemperate world are beyond the woods. They're out on the road, in the malls, or in the halls of the capitol. They are not on this path, at this bend, along this creek, in this stand of trees, fifty yards from that deer or crouching over this box turtle, in the veins on this leaf or in the sunbeam bouncing off the branches on its way to the ground.

Occasionally my mind would wander. I would stand for a moment in one spot and think of the millions of pairs of feet that had stood where I was, anonymous to me but known to others. Maybe those feet came once and never returned or maybe they made it back to that spot many, many times. Seeking or escaping? Alone or with others? I would wonder.

Maybe those feet grew larger as the years passed, clocking mile after mile, communing with nature (as the old saying goes). Or maybe those feet got busier with babies and bonuses and couldn't find the time to come again. Or maybe they grew weak and sore, along with knees and hips, and hiking boots were handed down or hung up so that their open tops would not spill the memories we reserve for "things" that are so much more than things.

At one time a young lover visiting Spider Woman had etched into the creek bed in paint and stone the message "Will You Marry Me?" Years of rain and runoff eventually washed away the proposal but I never fail to wonder, as I pass the familiar spot in those familiar woods, what the answer was. ☽

)

Spirits of Mepkin

There is something otherworldly about driving through the grand live oak allées of South Carolina lowcountry plantations: Boone Hall, Fenwick Hall, Brookgreen Gardens, Laurel Hill, and Brays Island. Motorcar notwithstanding, the ancient boughs of the trees seem to transport you to another time, another place, or perhaps, as Edgar Allan Poe said, "out of space, out of time." There is no allée grander or more transforming than that of Mepkin, for it is the gateway to a landscape layered in cultural diversity, swept by crosscurrents of South Carolina lowcountry history and life. To follow the road from the entryway down to the bluff that overlooks the Cooper River is to follow more or less the path Henry Laurens trod after purchasing the land in 1762.

Mepkin's beauty is haunting and haunted, with spirits all around. Henry Laurens, planter, patriot, president of the Continental Congress, was the first person of European descent to be cremated in North America. His funeral pyre was built on the high bluff above the riverbank, and his horrified former slaves watched in astonishment and terror as, legend has it, the head became separated from the body and rolled off down the road. If you listen carefully, you may hear the cadenced drumming tone, the rhythms of the Native American tribe, likely Wando, Etiwan, or Sewee, that first inhabited this land. The spirits of Henry Luce, cofounder and publisher of Time-Life, and Clare Booth Luce, congresswoman, diplomat, playwright, are palpable in their Loutrell Briggs–designed garden that so seamlessly melds nature and nurture.

This landscape of natural wonder tempered by human cultivation over hundreds of years bears the character and spirit of all the divergent, disparate peoples trusted with its stewardship. The present occupants, the

Brothers of the Order of Cistercians of the Strict Observance, continue in that tradition. Father Francis Kline, OCSO, the late abbot of Mepkin (1990–2006), said that a good steward of the land must keep the property intact, and know what happened there. He also said that Mepkin Abbey was like two rivers converged: one stream the Trappist tradition (named for the Norman abbey of La Trappe) begun in the sixth century by St. Benedict of Nursia; and the other stream, the cultural history of a Cooper River plantation from pre-Columbian times to the years of the Lords Proprietors, right through the ownership of Laurens and Luce.

The spirits of Mepkin, an assemblage of angels that seem omnipresent in the landscape, soothe my soul and bring me peace whenever I go there. For in "another" life, I am a neurological surgeon, and in that, the dichotomies of illness and health, life and death, can take their toll.

I had heard about Mepkin all my life but knew of it only as a strange Catholic religious house in Berkeley County. I do not suppose it ever occurred to my Presbyterian mother that there might have been some virtue in paying a visit. Nor was it so easy in the days before Father Francis, for the brothers pursued the contemplative life, cloistered, and largely insulated from their surroundings. Francis Kline brought Mepkin to the world, and the world to Mepkin. My wife knew him first, from her service on the abbey's foundation board. Jane had taken me to one of the lovely concerts and receptions the abbot hosted. I remain exceedingly grateful to her for that.

Soon after, I participated in a weekend retreat. Hoping to imitate the monastic life of the brothers in some small measure, I attended all the prayer services, which begin at 3:20 A.M. with Vigils and conclude at 7:30 P.M. with Compline. At the end of that office, all the monks and guests filed out of the church without a word as the Grand Silence commenced, to remain unbroken until the new cycle begins the next day. As I arrived at the portico, a shadowy figure in a monk's habit, hood over his head, beckoned. It was Abbot Francis, who as I approached whispered, "Would you like to meet with me this weekend?" Knowing the rule of the Grand Silence, I thought, "Is this some kind of test?" I nodded my assent, amid some confusion. Father Francis, like Mepkin itself, evinced his own sense of mystery. This became ever more manifest to me in the months and years to follow. And yes, that evening he was messing with me.

The name Mepkin (or Mebken as it appears in the earliest map of the region, dated 1696), is very likely Native American in origin. Across the river, on the site of Pimlico Plantation, stood "Mebshoo." Could the names mean right and left bank? One of the seven Lords Proprietors, John Colleton, had initial colonial charge of the property by royal land grant and passed it to his heirs until it was sold to Henry Laurens before the American Revolution. Clearly many African American slaves were bound to the Mepkin estate in the eighteenth and nineteenth centuries. The Rutgers family of New Jersey owned it briefly in the early twentieth century, until it was purchased by Henry and Clare Booth Luce in 1936. They left it to the Catholic Church and the Trappist brothers in 1949.

The bell tower, freestanding outside the abbey church, is known as the Tower of the Seven Spirits: of "the Indians, the Henry Laurens Family, the African Americans who worked the land, the Henry Luce family, the friends of the Abbey in the 'secular' cemetery, the monastic community in glory, and the monks who still remain on this earthly journey," as the dedication reads.

Elsewhere I have argued that art superimposes itself on geography and so transforms a literal place of experience into a risen place of the imagination. Mepkin is a paradigm of the transforming power of the imagination. The natural environment is interlaced with the vision of so many different cultural and historical perspectives. Here is the perfection of the lowcountry landscape in its Berkeley County form: moss-covered oaks, magnolias, cypresses, azaleas, yucca, elephant ears, palmetto trees, camellias, wisteria, and dogwoods. Here also are alligators, herons, snowy egrets, largemouth bass, and water moccasins. Terraces recall the estate's origins as a rice plantation, suggesting its extensive dike system, while the brothers work the land in the agricultural present, as did their Trappist forebears in Europe, as did the slaves and overlords that preceded them here and abroad. Remnants of the old "Slave Street" occupied by sharecroppers after Emancipation arrest the eye, and a slave graveyard lies silent in the woods.

This synthesis of cultures also is seen in the architecture. Winding through the monastic green are the ruins of the "serpentine" wall, the only reminder of the Henry Luce family home. Architect Edward Durell Stone worked at Mepkin for a time during the Luce years. The abbey church, designed in 1991 by architect Ted Butler and Frank Kacmarcik, Obl.S.B., is the centerpiece of the monastery. It evokes the character and simplicity of Trappist monasteries in twelfth-century France. And from the Luce years, there is the Briggs garden, when Mepkin became a refuge for the influential and famous of the time, and alleged trysts and affairs were legend.

Just off the bluff are submerged remains of the Mepkin dock, and farther out the Mepkin shipwreck, relics of commercial traffic with Charleston and reminders of how provisions moved in the eighteenth century. Just above

Mepkin Abbey Church.
Photograph by Tiffanie Daudelin.

the dock was the home of Henry Laurens, who was captured on the high seas while sailing to the Netherlands to secure aid for the revolutionary cause and imprisoned in the Tower of London. He was of such importance that he was later released in exchange for Lord Cornwallis. The simplicity of Laurens's plantation home is depicted in the several watercolors of Charles Frazier, from his *Charleston Sketchbook,* circa 1803, now in the Gibbes Museum of Art.

Francis Kline was as multifaceted as Mepkin itself. He was the man he needed to be for whatever constituency he was serving at the time, and the different aspects of his character were brought out by the personalities of the individuals whose lives he touched. By turns quiet, contemplative, and mysterious, he yet could be exuberant, enthusiastic, boyish, and funny. He had a zeal for life and all it holds (including some earthly things), and to me he was something of an epicure, a characteristic not generally associated with religious vocation. To the brothers he was a compassionate leader and a stalwart defender of the faith.

Francis and I traveled together, on one occasion, to the Trappist convent of Esperanza in Esmeraldas, Ecuador, which falls within Mepkin's "paternal" oversight. Our mission was to visit one of the sisters there, Gaien Escobar, who had previously come to South Carolina for treatment of a

brain tumor. On this house call in another hemisphere, we coped with a general strike and provincial rebellion that left us with the monumental task of finding a way from Quito to the coast, over the Andes Mountains through the road blocks of the Esmeraldan rebels. It was a major adventure that could have happened only with Francis. The beauty of the convent in Ecuador echoed Mepkin's. On a high bluff overlooking an estuary that empties into the Pacific, Esperanza's appearance and spirituality were much the same.

Francis was a runner. To be on time for the first prayer office of the day, he would rise around 2:30 A.M. for his morning run of several miles. In Ecuador, I joined him for the ritual and discipline of this early-morning exercise. He admonished me to stay behind him and on the elevated stone path that circulated through the monastery, and not to venture out into the high grass.

"Why is that?" I asked.

"Because otherwise the snakes will get you," he said with perfect comic timing and deadpan irony.

Francis Kline's legacy at Mepkin was born of a deep spiritual understanding and enormous intellectual appreciation of the Cistercian heritage. His knowledge base, particularly in the field of religious and cultural history, seemed nearly encyclopedic. But above all, he held a deep and abiding love for the arts: literature, architecture, fine arts, and especially music. He started his career as a professional concert organist before the contemplative life caught up with him. He suffused Mepkin with the arts and brought enrichment to the public by sponsoring countless classical music concerts, overseeing the architectural integrity of the monastery with its extensive building program, and over the years bringing to the abbey artistic treasures that ranged from the entire collection of his friend, the painter Ugo Tesoriere, to two deaccessioned sculptures from the Brooklyn Museum of Art: *Jesus and John (the Baptist),* by William Ordway Partridge, and *Mother Love,* by Emil Fuchs. The latter is a depiction of the martyrdom of St. Perpetua, which Francis himself said—with some delight—was "over the top" in its English Pre-Raphaelite excesses. Francis Kline also seemed to have read every book ever written and noted how inspiring Mepkin had been to writers. In one form or another Mepkin has been used as subject matter in literary works that include *A Day on Cooper River,* by John B. Irving; *The Vicar of Christ,* by Walter F. Murphy; *Beach Music,* by Pat Conroy; and *The Mermaid Chair,* by Sue Monk Kidd, among others.

During the 2013 dedication of Mepkin's new conference and retreat center, the late Francis Kline was heard once more. His performance on the Zimmer organ of Louie Vierne's "Final" from Symphony No. 1, digitally reproduced using a sequencer, reminded those assembled of his brilliance and virtuosity as a concert organist and of his energy and enthusiasm for life. It was as if his spirit were really there. Truly Mepkin's beauty is haunting, the spirits of Mepkin omnipresent.

In the year 2000 on a late fall day, my fourth child was baptized at Mepkin in a unique and beautiful ceremony. The service incorporated elements of Roman Catholic and English church traditions and was punctuated by a joyous procession outdoors around the abbey church. There was color, music, festivity, and glorification; the very landscape seemed to come more alive for the occasion.

Francis Kline was, as usual, his unrestrainedly exuberant self. It always seemed to me that his earthly journey was, at least in part, an inexhaustible celebration of life. It is this principle of life renewing itself—of resurrection—that Mepkin symbolizes, unifying so many cultures and traditions, the state of nature and civilization in a peace "which passes all understanding." ☽

☽

The Stillness of St. Thomas

Trees partially hide a striking church edifice along a busy Cainhoy Road in lower Berkeley County. A highway marker tells of the place locals call the Brick Church. It's just west of Cainhoy, an old port on the Wando River that flows to Charleston.

When autumn leaves fall, I slow my car for a glimpse and ponder its history. Sometimes I stop to commune with my ancestral spirits. Occasionally a motorist asks the resident caretaker why such a beautiful church stands so curiously alone. Others zoom past, unaware that centuries ago it was the center of this area's religious life and colonial-era politics.

The first church was erected in 1708, the highway marker says, but an 1815 fire destroyed it. Four years later, the current church rose on the existing foundation. The sign is too small for other interesting things—the violence it witnessed after the Civil War, the two wealthy men who aided it in times of need. St. Thomas Church presents many mysteries, but perhaps the most obvious is its positioning: why does the entrance face away from the highway?

I first became aware of St. Thomas in late 2004, after I began research for *Behind God's Back*. The book is a collection of memories of longtime Cainhoy, Wando, and Huger residents on the Cainhoy peninsula and nearby Daniel and St. Thomas islands. The area is inhabited primarily by descendants of enslaved people who have preserved an African-based culture called Gullah.

Commercial and residential expansion took off after the 1992 opening of the I-526 Expressway, much of it along Clements Ferry Road and on Daniel Island. With new people rapidly moving to Berkeley County, the Coastal Community Foundation asked me to document its history for newcomers

St. Thomas Church.
Painting by John W. Jones.

and especially long-term residents. *Behind God's Back* would remind them
that in spite of change, their history should not be forgotten.

Eddie Carson of Huger was one of the first interviewees. Back from
Columbia after a stint in the Marine Corps and retirement from the U.S.
Postal Service, Eddie was working as a community organizer and serving
on the board of the United Methodist Relief Center. In the Huger Community Center next to Cainhoy Elementary School, he opened a map and
patiently gave me one of my first lessons on the communities spread across
the Cainhoy peninsula and their relationship with area plantations.

Black people here are aware of their history, he said, because they
aren't that far removed from ancestors who were enslaved. They are a self-
sufficient and fiercely independent people who once farmed family-owned
land. If pushed too far, he added, they will quickly "let you know 'I am not
your slave.'"

Eddie's primer foreshadowed what I would soon encounter. On a driving tour we stopped at a granite mile marker along Cainhoy Road. Etched
into the stone are the number 12 and the word *Calais*. Mile markers noted

the distance between plantations, Eddie said. He didn't know the meaning of Calais, but he did know that Harry Frank Guggenheim altered the direction of Clements Ferry Road.

Then we went to the church, site of the "big gunfight." Caretaker Tammy Wilson Giannelli also referred to mile markers and Guggenheim, who owned the land around the church. Guggenheim had the old Clements Ferry Road that crossed his property closed to traffic, she said. Two more mile markers are on the property, and a third is nearby on Cainhoy Road, she informed. That incomplete history lesson gave clues to subjects requiring more study.

I learned New York industrialist Harry Frank Guggenheim bought several parcels in the Cainhoy area beginning in the early 1930s. Consolidating the property into a hunting retreat of more than ten thousand acres, he called it "Cain Hoy Plantation." It nearly encircled the church, which had fallen into misuse and disrepair, and was seldom used by the Episcopal diocese of South Carolina. By the mid-1950s, he'd had a portion of Clements Ferry Road on his land closed.

Old newspaper stories and letters in the Library of Congress prove Guggenheim's unmatched affection for the church that once served English and French-speaking worshipers in St. Thomas and St. Denis Parish. French Protestants settled on nearby French Quarter Creek. By the late 1930s, Guggenheim began a three-decade effort to protect the church.

In the spring of 1960, Guggenheim wrote to the Right Reverend Thomas N. Carruthers, the diocesan bishop, to express his fondness and support for the church. Guggenheim suggested a trust fund for the sanctuary. On June 12, 1960, Carruthers died. In May 1962 Guggenheim wrote to Bishop Gray Temple, Carruthers's successor, for permission to endow a fund for the church. "The church is a lovely example of colonial architecture. It has great charm and beautiful simplicity of lines within and without. The graveyard is of historic interest. . . . One of the desecrated graves contains the remains of the principal benefactor of the Church and Parish, Richard Beresford."

Planter Richard Beresford was an early supporter of the parish and the Anglican church. His life cut short by a falling limb in 1722, Beresford's estate expanded education for the parish's poor children. On a bluff overlooking the Wando in Cainhoy, the parish built Beresford House, a three-story schoolhouse and rectory. Beresford's estate created the "Beresford Bounty" as continuous support for the school. The diocese still manages the fund.

Guggenheim may have followed Beresford's lead when on Christmas Day 1962 he established a fund to assist the church. He endowed it with

$10,000 and contributed $1,000 more for immediate repairs. In the ensuing years, vandalism and deterioration outpaced repairs and the diocese's interest. Through his attorney, Henry B. Smythe of Charleston, Guggenheim reminded diocesan leaders the fund was established to benefit the St. Thomas Church and not other colonial-era churches. By 1969 Guggenheim and the fund's trustees had grown frustrated by the diocese's apathy. The fund matured to slightly more than $16,000, but the trustees contemplated eliminating it if the diocese was not willing to oversee repairs and hold more services there.

Through the church's history, services were intermittent and sometimes suspended during the "unhealthiness" of the summer climate. By the early 1900s, the parish had become dormant and services infrequent. In January 1971 Guggenheim died at age eighty. The trust's assets in 1999 were transferred to the diocese.

Guggenheim's papers do not immediately explain why a northerner cared more for a southern colonial-era church than its owners. Was Guggenheim following his family's history of philanthropy? Or was he inspired by Beresford's generosity more than two centuries ago?

Although a marble tablet inside the church says he's buried there, I've failed to find Beresford's headstone. He's likely interred in the Beresford family tomb next to the church—yet another mystery St. Thomas hasn't given up.

Former caretaker John Clayton told me that hidden among the trees is the remnant of a post that supported a bandstand used during a political rally that sparked the gunfight. I haven't found it. Newspapers and federal records document that bloody chapter in the parish's history.

After the Civil War people of African descent enjoyed huge political gains. But dramatic racial violence also occurred. Preceding the 1876 gubernatorial election, violence reached Cainhoy on October 16 at the political rally attended by white Democrats and black Republicans. Both sides agreed to come unarmed, but black people had reason to be cautious. Already that year, whites had killed blacks during riots in Hamburg and Ellenton. Many blacks brought shotguns and muskets, which they hid in the woods and near the bandstand.

During the fiery rhetoric a shot rang out. Democrats ran, seeking safety at the Beresford House. Others fell wounded. Federal troops restored order, and the governor ordered an investigation. A federal inquiry concluded whites fired first. The *News and Courier* denounced the federal report as a "suppression of truth and downright misstatements."

Jim Alston, a former slave at the Hampton Plantation on the South Santee River, had stood next to John Lachicotte, the only black victim. In a 1926 story in the *News and Courier,* Alston said whites shot first, killing Lachicotte. The white victims were Thomas Whitaker, William E. Simmons, Alexander McNeil, William Daly, J. King, and Walter Gradick.

Black Cainhoy residents were perceived to have won. To some, it was a matter of black resistance to white attacks; to others it was unjustified black violence. The gunfight is unusual in the state's history of racial confrontations during Reconstruction because blacks won. The roadside marker at the church does not mention the gunfight.

Although I didn't find the bandstand's post, I saw a dirt road that was once the well-traveled Clements Ferry Road. The church faces the old road that stopped at a ferry landing on Daniel Island. There, commuters took the ferry to the upper end of the Charleston peninsula called the Neck. Travelers called it the "Dover and Calais" ferry, a joking comparison the English and French parishioners made to the English Channel ferry between Dover, England, and Calais, France. Mile markers along Clements Ferry Road noted the distance to the ferry.

I wanted to tell Eddie and other residents more of their history than they already knew. I also hoped to find my history. My paternal grandmother, Mable McNeil Frazier, came from Cordesville, just north of Huger. I didn't find her parents, Joseph and Elizabeth McNeil of St. Thomas Parish, or evidence to show whether their parents were enslaved or free. The search continues.

Parish records provide a detailed yet limited history of the church and the names of the parish's English and French residents. In the stillness of the white-walled sanctuary, I've wondered if parish records might yield the names of the free blacks and enslaved, maybe providing a clue to my ancestors who lived some distance from the church. The records promised to tell me more. Two volumes are said to hold a few names of "free negroes" and records of the baptisms, confirmations, communions, marriages, and burials of many slaves. I've looked carefully, but the names aren't there. The slave owners' names are listed, but the enslaved are forgotten.

It is regrettable that Grandmother never spoke of her Cordesville past, and I was too young to ask. When she took me to church in the city, she would remind me that church is a place for quiet meditation. The stillness at St. Thomas Church reminds me of her words.

While I have not yet found my kin, I want to believe that in the stillness of St. Thomas Church I found my ancestors' spirits. I want to believe they too were self-sufficient and fiercely independent. I want to believe that had my ancestors from Cordesville been at the rally, they too would have defended themselves. I want to believe that if they had been provoked that day in 1876, they would have said: "I am not your slave." ☽

Christopher Dickey

Pilgrimage

The two headstones stand beneath enormous old live oaks, and I sometimes try to imagine what it would be like to lie there looking up at the sky day after day, night after night, through the tangled threads of Spanish moss and the gray-green leaves that know no seasons. The branches cast their cool shadows even in the hot wet heat of summer. The sun moves in its arc behind the thin mist rising from the marshes, and at night the stars spread out like sugar across the sky. Orion rises and turns around and around, slowly searching for his way home from the hunt.

Those who do lie here do not see, of course. The caskets are closed, and the earth weighs heavily on top of them. But still one imagines so many things in such a place. Country churchyards, far from the madding crowd, are magnificent for imagining, and long before my mother and my father were buried here, I would come to walk among the stones that remembered some of the men and women and little children who peopled the rice plantations nearby.

In a far corner, bedeviled by teenagers frightening themselves into each other's embrace, a woman lies beneath a large stone that bears the name "Alice." Around it the ground is deeply worn by the ritual circles turned in the dark of night to raise the spirit of a girl whose love and life ended too soon. But I have never walked that circle. Alice is not the ghost I am looking for.

My mother, in a moment typical of her organizational foresight, bought four plots in the old churchyard of All Saints Waccamaw at Pawleys Island. She had joined the congregation because she loved the lowcountry so much, and belonging to a church is part of belonging to a place. We only ever went to Pawleys for a few days or weeks at a time, but those cemetery plots created a notion of permanence. One was for her, one for my father, one for my brother, and one for me. None of us expected we'd reside there at All Saints in any near future. We boys were just teenagers back then, and our parents seemed far too young to die, but we all took some sort of vague comfort from the tranquil beauty of the place. And then, too suddenly and too soon, my mother did die.

Maxine Syerson Dickey, 1926–1976, was buried beneath the stone with a little owl on it, a chiseled impression of the famous watercolor by Albrecht Durer that art historians call "the essence of owlness." The epitaph, chosen by my father, is from a verse by the sixteenth-century poet Henry Constable:

I do love thee as each flower
Loves the sun's life-giving power.

My father did not include the next line of that stanza, although he must have had it in mind: "For dead, thy breath to life might move me."

Dickey Family gravesite.
Photograph by Megan Sexton.

A little more than twenty years later, when the lichens had colored the edges of my mother's stone, my father joined her. On his stone there is an eye peering through pine branches, a motif he had designed for the cover of the first edition of his first novel, *Deliverance*. And now the lichens and the mist have lent their patina to his stone as well.

From time to time tourists pass by All Saints, and a guide tells them that the famous poet and novelist James Dickey is buried here, but when I have chanced to be present for such a visit I have seen the lack of recognition in their eyes. The paths of glory soon get lost in the weeds. The public moves on. But some people do remember. People whom I do not know leave flowers on the graves. Some of the blossoms are bought from a florist, some are picked wild along the roadside. Visitors leave single feathers that drifted off the wings of gulls hovering above the beach. They leave sea shells.

My own ritual, when I come to this most beautiful corner of South Carolina, is very simple. I brush aside the little threads of Spanish moss that have fallen on top of the stones and, lightly, just for a moment, I kiss the granite of each one. It is cool, and solid, and enduring. Then I look up at the branches and the sun above, and I imagine Orion in the night. The hunt is over. ☽

Eulalie Salley, Age Sixteen.
Photograph courtesy of Emily Cooper, from her book *Eulalie.*

Feminine Expression

"Every man in town turned against me and a lot of my family was against me. They thought I had disgraced the family. They thought it was outrageous, that only bad women, prostitutes, were suffragists."

Aiken businesswoman Eulalie Salley (1883–1975), who opened her real estate company in 1915 and became president of the South Carolina Equal Suffrage League in 1919.

From *Documenting the American South,* University Library of the University of North Carolina at Chapel Hill

Glenis Redmond

)

Dancing between Worlds

South Carolina–born, I was military-raised on Air Force bases across the country and in Europe. These military jaunts most likely account for the reason I did not make the immediate connection between the Charleston, the dance, to my own South Carolina roots. Obviously the dance held some innate key, because I could always be found up on my toes, feet twisting into that quirky kick. First forward. Then back. My fingers splayed, circling to the left and then to the right, while singing the lyrics that go with the dance: Charleston, Charleston / Made in South Carolina.

At nine I was happy just to find joy in this jig. I was a kinesthetic wunderkind, completely entranced. It would take me many years to comprehend the deepness of my connection to South Carolina. Looking back I cannot help but think I was always Carolina kissed and claimed.

Daddy was from Fountain Inn, and Mama was from Waterloo, and I was the only one of their five offspring born in their native state. Sumter was where I made my entry: more specifically, Shaw Air Force Base. The genesis of my groove began there—most likely in my mama's womb—moving in time with her Sunday morning church pew sway. I think it is understandable that dance is how I pray.

In my childhood home I had plenty of opportunity to talk to God, because Daddy played the piano. With his music he rocked our household hard with his jazz, blues, and gospel music. He played by ear, and I danced—danced and danced.

No matter where we moved on our Air Force trek—Washington state, Italy, or New Jersey—the places that made me feel most at home were not places on a map, but in the pages of books or in the throes of dance. Dance was my first love—before words, before poetry. It was my one true constant, where I felt most surefooted, where I did not have to ask any questions. In dance I did not need anyone's instruction or permission. I felt like a winged being.

When Daddy wasn't wrapping the house in song, our record player always had vinyl on spin. I grew up to the soundtrack of 1960s and '70s music: James Brown; the Staple Singers; the Ohio Players; Earth, Wind and Fire; the Spinners; Sly and the Family Stone; and the old-school list goes on and on.

I was a Jackson Five fan, and their album *Lookin' Through The Windows* was one of my first prized possessions. I danced to "Dancing Machine" frequently, and I fantasized that Michael was singing directly to me. When he chanted "watch her get down, watch her get down," I did.

I was a teenager before I realized that everyone did not grow up with music and dancing 24/7. Though we lived below the poverty line, we were culturally rich. I never felt like I came from lack. I am sure my parents, who did their best to give us what they had, were more aware of poverty's clench. Ironically, our poor was the richest they had ever been, having both come from sharecropping lineages.

Subsequently, I was a Head Start kid in 1967. At four my sister Velinda, six years my senior, took me to the Head Start's afterschool program in Tacoma, Washington. On Wednesdays in a school gymnasium, I came alive in a room full of batons, hula hoops, jump ropes, and music. My relationship with dance deepened when I learned modern, jazz, and interpretive. How the Charleston first entered my life is unknown, but it claimed me, or I claimed it. It was as if I just came knowing how to do it.

Supposedly I was steeped in a rich collective history. But my specific lineage had many missing pieces: one, because of our military wanderings, and two, because slavery stunted and thwarted African American history and my education did little to inform me of what did exist.

Then it seemed Charleston outstretched its arm of memory asking me to dance and gave me the answers to my origin story.

I felt the pull.

In 1991 I moved back to South Carolina from Virginia where my twins were born. My husband at the time and I went to Charleston on our fifth anniversary. The trip was supposed to be a celebration, but Charleston had much more to show me beyond Rainbow Row, cobblestone roads, shopping, and lowcountry eating. In my poem "Praise Dave," I write about how a place can carry simultaneous stories.

Even my empty pots
be full. One say:
I wonder where is all my relations
Friendship to all—and every nation.
There are lanterns in my words—
every story got another story.

I unearth David Drake's voice in this persona poem. The enslaved potter/poet from Edgefield, South Carolina, speaks passionately about our African American stories lest they are forgotten or go untold.

As I walked in Charleston, I watched the women on the corners weaving sweetgrass with their deft hands. To me they were braiding the West Coast of Africa with the Carolina shores, connecting my histories in ways I had never witnessed. Yet, as quickly as my past was coming together, I seemed to be coming undone.

On a carriage tour, every bump on the cobblestones seemed to throw me to the past, just as Dana was thrown back to antebellum times in Octavia Butler's *Kindred*. I started convulsing. It was a nonepileptic seizure, but I felt quaked awake and began speaking in an unknown tongue. About five years later, I wrote about that experience in a poem titled "If I Ain't African."

If I ain't African
how come my feet do an African dance?
How come every time
I'm in New Orleans-Charleston I fall into a trance?

Out of its port-city mouth Charleston spoke, and I listened. I sensed the pitch and moan of those enslaved. I heard the sorrow of the auction-block song. Though I quickly came back to the present, my vantage point had shifted in an instant. My awareness of where I came from was heightened and forever altered on that trip.

It felt like a sort of literary and cultural initiation. Charleston whispered in my ear, and I began my poetic journey of stitching a continent to a state. Wherever I looked in South Carolina, there always seemed to be a thread of Africa—even in the Charleston dance.

I had always associated the dance to the white flappers of the 1920s. When I researched it, I found that two African Americans, Cecil Mack and James P. Johnson, created the song and dance. Joseph E. Holloway's book *Africanism in American Culture* explains that Africans brought the dance to

The author getting down after a book release party in the Chicago Cultural Center ballroom, 2012. Photograph by Syreeta McFadden.

America from the Congo between 1735 and 1740. In Africa it was danced as a one-legged Sembuka: an over-and-cross step. African Americans adapted the steps and made it their own. It then became known in the black community as the Juba Dance. When it crossed over to the mainstream, white America fell in love with it. The dance gained fame and became known as the Charleston.

On that same trip, I picked up Elizabeth Nunez-Harrell's *When Rocks Dance*. The book's cover drew me: black women dancing with hips in midswing. It felt as if the ancestors guided me to this book, because when I turned to the back, an excerpt read:

"You have forgotten the old ways.
You don't come to worship here.
Your mother, she was loyal.
She never forgot Africa."

In Charleston I could feel the cobblestone roads shift beneath me. With the music, tongue, dance, and drum, and the power of the ancestors, I was dancing between the worlds. In hindsight it seems that when I was nine dancing the Charleston, I was unknowingly dancing to a deeper dance. I was connecting to my ancestry. Perhaps it was a foretelling of my path, and these were the steps that would lead to Charleston, my genius loci, a place spiritually loaded for me.

Even the Angel Oak, with her fifteen-thousand-year-old self, made me feel embraced. When I spied a white squirrel scampering tree to tree, following our car down the dirt road, I made my friend stop driving so I could document the moment. Later I read the myth of the white squirrel: it is the guardian of the tree.

Of course, I took it as a sign, but I am a poet, and I am susceptible to signs. Yet the mystic in me says there are no accidents and that synchronistic moments are grace washing upon my shore, nudging me into a deeper knowing, urging me to pay attention to the stories held in the land.

Charleston is my favorite place because more than any other place it connects me to who I am—a South Carolinian with deep African roots, roots that insist on dancing me to deeper levels. I have accepted the invitation. I have taken the hand of this holy city that is possessed with history. I will not let it go, because here is where I am most embraced and made most whole. ☽

)

Prodigal Daughter

When I made the impulsive decision to go back to church after two decades in the heathen wilderness, I bypassed the pews and headed straight for the choir loft. It was music, not religion, that brought me to First Presbyterian in downtown Beaufort a little more than seven years ago.

I grew up in Alabama, where my parents raised us Methodist. They sent my sisters and me to Sunday school, MYF, Camp Sumatanga, the works. Despite their diligence, it never really took. I stopped going to church in college at Sewanee, where I didn't so much "lose my faith" as discover I didn't have any. All it took was a little book learnin'—and a few late-night keg parties—and I was done getting up early on Sunday mornings for something that seemed both unlikely and irrelevant. Later I went to grad school at the University of Alabama to study English. It was the late 1980s, deconstruction was all the rage, and the bias against religion was palpable in our department. To an insecure young scholar, the message came through loud and clear: you're either a thinker or a believer; you can't be both. I took that message to heart and lived it, rather religiously, for twenty years.

But I never got over the music. My parents had sung in the church choir; they'd brought us up to love Bach and Beethoven, Schubert and Handel. That stuff gets in your bones, your blood. Faith may desert you, but music doesn't.

So there I was one cold morning in December, sitting in First Presbyterian Church of Beaufort—some friends had invited me—listening to the choir sing the Christmas part of Handel's *Messiah* . . . and crying like a baby. Something happened to me that morning, and I still don't understand it. I heard the words I'd heard a thousand times before—*And the government shall be upon his shoulder, and his name shall be called Wonderful Counselor, the Mighty God, the Everlasting Father, the Prince of Peace*—and my heart just cracked wide open. Suddenly, I wanted to believe those words more than anything in the world, and I wanted that music to go on forever. When the performance ended, I marched my shaken, trembling self up to the choir director—a total stranger—and asked if I could join his group. It was the most impetuous thing I'd ever done. Had I given it even a moment's thought, I'd have talked myself out of it. I've since learned that Christians call this "stepping out on faith." It felt more like walking the plank. I was terrified.

Fast-forward seven years. I am a second soprano. I sit on the second row, near the middle of the choir loft, where I spend a lot of time studying the back of my minister's head. Patrick is a youngish man—early forties—and I like the way his thick black hair swirls neatly above his collar. In summer, he wears an alb made of rough white cloth, with a fat rope at the waist. This monastic touch moves me, though I'm not sure why. I like hearing Patrick read scripture, his voice deep and resonant, without a trace of twang. I like that his sermons are thoughtful and challenging, that he quotes C. S. Lewis and Henri Nouwen, Martin Luther King and Bono. I sometimes wish he'd give easier answers—would tell me exactly what to be believe, and how— but I also know a preacher like that would soon drive me nuts . . . and right back out of the church.

It was in the choir loft that I shocked myself by remembering every single word of the Apostles' Creed. It just came flooding back, line by line, after twenty years in mental exile. Same for the Lord's Prayer, the Doxology, the Gloria Patri. I spent that first Sunday in the choir loft almost too overwrought to speak *or* sing. The words kept rushing back like long lost friends—who knew I'd missed them?—and my throat would tighten, then the tears would come. So I just listened, mostly; I'm not sure I'd ever really listened before. What splendid words they were! It felt so strange to be there, both audacious and humbling. (Who did I think I was, after all this time away?) But it felt right, too. Like coming home. I felt like the prodigal daughter.

From the choir loft, I can see everything—humanity in all its terrible beauty. Old men sleeping, young children squirming, teenagers snickering, new mothers joggling infants, rushing out when the wailing starts. I see women wobbling in on ridiculous heels and men checking their watches and kids doodling on their bulletins during the pastoral prayer. From the choir loft, everyone looks small and vulnerable, and I love them all. Mercy comes easy in the choir loft.

First Presbyterian Church, Beaufort.
Photograph courtesy of the author.

Sometimes, after the prayer of confession, I can even extend it to myself.

I like watching the congregation walk forward to take Communion. The sight of all those ordinary people in their contemporary clothes slowly moving forward for this ancient sacrament just gets to me. *People still do this. After two thousand years.* "Great is the mystery of faith," reads the minister. I watch as the people pinch bread from the loaf, dip it in the cup, return to their pews, lower their heads. I wonder what they're thinking, what they're feeling. *The body and blood of Christ.* What does that mean to them? To me?

Presbyterians are big on their Scottish heritage, and from the choir loft the annual Kirkin' of the Tartans is dazzling to behold. I'll never forget my first Kirkin' processional as it came toward me down the aisle—the men in their kilts and women in their sashes, the tartan flags held high, the mournful drone of bagpipes. When the service ended and the processional headed back to the narthex, I caught sight of Reverend Miller and Bishop Hathaway from our neighbor church, St. Helena's—the bishop in full Anglican regalia, looking damn near papal—standing on the sidewalk outside our doors, waiting to parade with us through the streets of downtown Beaufort.

The Anglicans were resplendent in the bright fall sunshine, and the image of them framed in our Presbyterian doorway is a permanent snapshot in my memory.

From my perch in the choir loft, it's always wonderful to see our doors thrown open to the street outside. It happens every Easter, just before we end with the "Hallelujah Chorus." The ushers open the doors, we choristers rise, the familiar strains of Handel's joyous anthem begin, and the whole congregation stands. It's taken me years of practice to sing over the lump that inevitably fills my throat. Handel brought me back to church, and Handel's one reason I stick around. But not the only reason.

It was in the choir loft that we sang "Holy, Holy, Holy" with all of Old Beaufort at Helen Harvey's funeral. It was her favorite hymn—she adored the descant, and I swear there were angels singing it with us that day. It was from the choir loft that I heard Pat Conroy eulogize his dear friend and "second mother" Julia Randell, and there that I've sung the 23rd Psalm at more funerals than I can count. I've watched children weeping for their lost fathers from that choir loft, and mothers crying over their newly baptized babies.

Sometimes I sit looking out at our sanctuary, so simple and austere (though I'm told there are more than twenty different shades of white paint in that room), and I miss the baroque church of my childhood—its dark, ornate carvings and flamboyant stained-glass windows. I don't know that I'm a Presbyterian at heart; I'm certainly not a Calvinist. If it were just about aesthetics, I'd probably be a High Church Catholic. If it were just about theology, well, who knows? I'm not sure it's all that important. If God is Love, I've found him here in this little white church in downtown Beaufort.

I still have all the old questions; I still struggle with belief. I probably make it a lot harder than it needs to be—once a thinker, always a thinker. But the choir loft is a very good place to hash it out. Or better yet, just to let it be. In the choir loft, I can rest with my questions. I can silence all those voices that vie for attention in my beleaguered brain—the critic, the cynic, the anxious preteen, the spoiled brat—and I can cultivate something akin to peace. Peace! And sometimes, if I don't screw it up, I think I can even hear the voice of God.

And what it sounds like . . . is music. ↄ

Boy cane pole fishing on the Lynches River, Lee State Park. Courtesy of the South Caroliniana Library, University of South Carolina, Columbia, S.C.

Currents

Oh, we did enjoy those nights on the river bank. Wouldn't carry a thing with us but what clothes we had on, a frying pan, and fishing pole. After we had caught all the fish we wanted, we would make up a big fire to cook the fish and tell stories around. I did love to lie there and listen to the owls hoot and hear the river water running in the bushes.

Farmer Wilbur White (fictitious name John Black) of Marion County to Annie Ruth Davis, South Carolina Writers' Project, 1938

A Long Time Afloat on the Great Santee

There is something forceful and majestic about the surging power of our rivers as they near the terminus of their long runs and begin to compete with the salt and the tides. The rivers I chiefly patrolled during my game warden days included the Ashepoo, Combahee, Edisto, Stono, Wando, Santee, and the Ashley and Cooper. All but the last two are named for Indian tribes that lived around those streams during the Carolina colony's settlement. Along with their tribal names, ancient structures called shell rings—scenes of ancient barbecues and oyster roasts scattered along the coastal plain—bear mute testimony to their former habitation.

It was always interesting to consider that I often was traveling the same routes and enjoying the same wild vistas as our earliest citizens. A stretch of the lower Santee River roughly ten miles long and two miles wide is where I spent most of my river time. At the topside of that reach, at the point where the river has followed its course through the state for some four hundred miles, the river splits into the North and South Santee. The prodigious effects of the tide on the river extend some thirty-eight miles upstream to Highway 41 at Jamestown.

Where the river divides, the North Santee continues broad and strong on its winding journey to the sea. The southern course enters a narrow, tree-shrouded channel fraught with snags and obstructions. The Francis Marion National Forest guards its western shoulder, and then it passes Hampton Plantation, the ancestral home of the great Archibald Rutledge, whose poetry and prose about the Santee River fills volumes.

Even while keeping a sharp lookout for perils just beneath the inky surface, there was still time to absorb the scenic rewards of this untamed and beautiful area. The Santee offers a constantly changing, seasonal palette. Along the south channel the delicate springtime greenery of the soaring cypress, gums, and pines gives way in the fall to paint-box red, yellow, and purple leaves that dapple the surface of the water and settle on the forest floor. In the winter, it takes on the likeness of a black-and-white picture, sere and leafless. I frequently shut off the skiff's engine and drifted with the current, where all I could hear was the liquid whisper of the rushing water and the breezes passing through the outstretched branches above.

Good as that was, it was the dramatic coastal landscape downstream, the Santee delta, that consumed most of my attention. The delta is a continuous progression of plantation rice field impoundments jutting out from the mainland and standing shoulder to shoulder along the banks of both rivers, from Highway 17 to the ocean. In their heyday, the plantations functioned as one big hydraulic instrument with dikes and elaborate water control structures called trunks, which harnessed the force of the tide to irrigate the crop.

Along with the trunks, the original designs of which are still used today, the great system of dikes, canals, ditches, and drains bear witness to the transformative efforts and facility of the Negro slaves, who dug out swampland and salt marsh mud, creating what became part of one of the great agricultural operations in America.

After the Civil War, the rice fields fell into disrepair, beaten down by climate, credit, and competition. In the last decades of the nineteenth century and well into the first half of the twentieth, the plantations were "rescued" by northern duck hunters who acquired them, restored the dikes, and cultivated indigenous aquatic vegetation—not rice—to attract and hold ducks. The management efforts of private and state owners made the delta one of the finest magnets for overwintering waterfowl on the East Coast. It's hugely attractive to hunters plying the public waters around the plantations.

The waterfowlers were, by no means, the sole cause of my official presence there. The Santee also saw seasonal traffic of fishermen setting gill nets for shad, and before it was made illegal, netting for the imposing Atlantic sturgeon. It was also one of the very few areas of the South Carolina coast where large funnel-shaped channel nets could legally be set to catch shrimp. My fellow wardens and I also rode herd on an active flotilla of crabbers whose colorful pot markers dotted the channels across the delta. At one time the Santee's lower reaches were a rich source of true single oysters and beds of clams so thick it took a mechanical harvester to handle the numbers. All of those activities were regulated, which is why I was there sniffing about.

My direct encounters with duck hunters and watermen were usually quite brief, leaving plenty of time for exploring the myriad little watercourses lacing through the broad plains of dense marsh grass. To get the best view, I would climb from my skiff to the top of a dike, where I sometimes perched for hours behind a patch of grass just looking and listening, waiting for something to happen.

I was always pleasantly surprised and privately delighted when my patience paid off, and the careless or greedy got to carry home some paper. Among other dividends to reap, if I kept still long enough, was observing the procession of raccoons, mink, cotton rats, and otter. Birds of every description—waterfowl, wading birds, bald eagles, and swallow-tailed kites—scurried, stalked, soared, or hunted prey, unaware of their enraptured audience. There was also the dependable presence of swimming or slithering reptiles to ensure I didn't doze off too deeply.

Out there on the river there were times I experienced feelings of infinitesimal smallness, particularly when the coal-black clouds of a thunderstorm roared over me like a stampede. They often came with hail, freezing cold downdrafts, huge pelting raindrops, and close lightning strikes that sounded like giant panes of shattering glass. In those vast open expanses of marsh, there was no place to hide. When those thunderstorms hit, I resorted to my Br'er Fox routine: I "lay low."

At first traversing the delta through the predawn shadows was spooky, but eventually the silhouettes of the shoreline became familiar landmarks. According to the tide, I could find one of my holes in the grass to conceal my skiff and play the seasonal reenactment of grown-up Hide and Seek. Peering over the marsh grass, I was a frequent witness to spectacularly brilliant sunrises. I was also there many mornings and evenings when clouds, rain, or fog hid the sun, masking unseen miscreants who would do their mischief. Never mind, I knew anybody out there had to come back right by me.

Hidden in that lower delta were vine-clad brick foundations of rice-era structures. In certain places beneath the high tide, piles of ballast stones and slave-made bricks occasionally revealed themselves on the ebb. One mid-delta impoundment contained the circular remains of an old brick storm tower adapted for use by a duck club.

Another, farther seaward, didn't fare as well: its remoteness made it vulnerable to vandalism, and its proximity to salt air caused deterioration.

Moreland Plantation storm tower on the Santee delta.
Photograph courtesy of the author.

Three islands—Cedar, Murphy, and South—stand sentinel where the North and South Santee rivers meet the sea. Once home to isolated slave settlements and remote postbellum summer retreats, Murphy and Cedar now are uninhabited. On their seaward sides, they look much as they did when the first European colonists arrived, minus the sea level differences. I could only imagine the tedium of their forays into the delta without anything like modern day "Bug Juice" to ward off the world-class swarms of mosquitoes, ticks, deer flies, red bugs, and no-see-ums, all of which have been vigilantly searching for fresh blood supplies for thousands of years.

Two miles of the Atlantic Intracoastal Waterway intersect both rivers and stretch across the middle of the lower delta. Its commercial and recreational boat traffic reminded me I was still in the modern world. The strident throb of diesel engines and the roar of their wakes marked their noisy passage across the delta's otherwise solemn quietude.

To really get to know that territory and be comfortable in it, in darkness and light and all stages of the tide, takes time. Over the seasons I got to know most of the people who hunted or fished there and when they would come and where they would go. I learned who appeared to belong and who didn't quite fit the picture. The people I encountered in my "office"—the hunters, landowners, and watermen—were the spice of my daily patrols, a constant source of "educational" moments and unending lessons in the foibles of human nature.

It has been a few years since I last circled the Santee delta, investigating the arabesque interconnecting channels, walking atop the impoundments, exploring the adjacent woodlands and barrier islands. But in quiet moments, I can close my eyes and follow every bit of it just as well as that day I stepped out of the boat from my last patrol. It is remarkable to think I spent almost twenty-five years working in that splendid landscape with the waters of the great Santee River running under my boat. ☽

)

Lowcountry Tides

All man's pollutions doth the salt sea cleanse.

Euripides

You're eight years old, and your grandfather died this morning. You're pissed off at God, and your sadness steals your breath. You run from the house toward the creek after you hear the news. You lie on your stomach feeling the weathered boards of the dock beneath you, and watch fiddler crabs scurry in the pluff mud until your tears subside, and the skittish fiddlers emerge from their holes and resume their crabby activities. The fiddlers with the large claws used to scare you, but now you know how to grab them by that one big claw so they won't pinch you. Your older sister taught you how to do that and also that the ones with the single large claws are the boy fiddlers. You lie there until Church Creek rises and fills the crab holes. You watch, thinking about your grandfather and God, and wonder if you can now talk to Granddaddy by praying, the way you talk to God. You decide you can, and so you close your eyes and think all the thoughts you want your grandfather to know. You tell him about the fiddlers.

You're thirteen. You're at your best friend's house, and you've spent the day on the Kiawah River pulling each other on the kneeboard behind the johnboat. If you'd been at your house you'd have been on Church Creek or the Bohicket River doing the same thing. You putter a little farther down the river than you ever have before, and you discover a small island with a narrow strip of sandy beach. You and your friend pull the boat up and toss the anchor onto the sand. You spread your towels and drink Cokes from the little cooler you've brought and talk about high school boys, your junior varsity basketball team, where you'll go to college, and how you'll decorate your dorm room when you're roommates. The tide goes out, but by the time you notice, the boat is high and dry. Shoving the boat down to the water takes the two of you over an hour. That evening your muscles ache and you're brown as a berry, but you sleep like only a thirteen-year-old can sleep and vow to tell no one about your secret island. You plan to return there many more times, but the summer races by, and you never go there again. You can't imagine that you and your best friend will go to different colleges where you each room with people neither of you knew when you were thirteen. Nor can you know then that on your road trips to the low-country from Clemson University you'll always lower the car window when you near the Ashley River regardless of the weather to inhale the briny scent of home.

You're seventeen and you have a boyfriend, and he loves the river as much as you do. It's late June, and the dolphin fish are biting. You know when you speak to tourists from Ohio or Kentucky at the restaurant on Big Bay Creek at Edisto Beach where you wait tables that you must say *mahi mahi* when referring to a dolphin fish, or else the tourists will freak out and think they're eating Flipper. You, your boyfriend, and his father leave the Intracoastal Waterway before sunrise and make your way offshore to where the Gulfstream flows, and you rig the ballyhoo and feel something you sus-pect is akin to the exuberance a mullet feels when he jumps in the ebbing tide. You could almost cry at the beauty of the brilliant sky and the mystery of flying fish that somehow go the length of a football field before submerg-ing, and a sea so slick it's like blue oil. When you hook a thirty-pound dol-phin and witness that beautiful green-blue-yellow creature explode through the water forty yards from the boat, you cannot believe such a powerful gorgeous thing is on your line, and you reel-reel-reel until your forearm might burst, but you know if you don't get him to the boat all by yourself the catch doesn't count as your catch. That night your mama fries the pink fillets and serves them with creamy grits and Wadmalaw Island tomatoes, and you suspect you'll marry that boy who took you fishing.

You're twenty-five, and you arrive home from a weekend in Spartanburg wearing a diamond and ruby ring on your left ring finger. You're engaged to a boy from the upstate. Daddy tells people that you're marrying a Yankee since your intended hails from north of Orangeburg County. You're excited and nervous, but mostly you're just extraordinarily happy. A know-it-all neighbor from down the road says to your father within earshot of you, "That marriage ain't gonna last. That gal can't handle living away from the salt marsh." You want to punch him, but later, at the day's gloaming, you sit alone on the dock dangling your feet in the cool green-brown water, watching a periwinkle snail work its way up a stalk of Spartina as the tide slowly floods and blue herons head to the far trees to roost, and, though you love your Spartanburg boy more than just about anything, you secretly fear that the loudmouth from down the road is on to something.

You're thirty-six and you just had your third child at Spartanburg Regional Hospital, and you name him William after your maternal grandfather, who, like eight generations before him, lived on the sea islands of South Carolina and knitted his own cast nets. Your other two children are girls, two and a half and six, and you are adamant that (1) you will always send Christmas card photos of your children, and (2) the photos must be taken in the South Carolina lowcountry. When you tell your babies bedtime stories the tales do not come from books but from your memories of days spent as a feral child hauling shrimp and mullet in the cast net and of catching blue crabs with your brothers using chicken necks for bait and selling the crabs three bucks a dozen. You tell of bogging in creek mud and getting oyster cuts on your bare feet and exploring islands

The author with her father, son, and parents' dog on Garden Creek, a tributary of the Toogoodoo River, just south of Yonges Island. Photograph courtesy of Michel Stone.

in johnboats. Your stories are such that on the rare occasion when you pull a book from the shelf for a bedtime story the children shriek in protest. "No! No," they say. "Tell us about when you were a girl! Tell us about the lowcountry!"

You are forty-three, and your parents say they need to figure out their wills. You want to say, "Don't talk like that! You're not going anywhere!" But you know such planning is prudent. You have three siblings who all live in the lowcountry, but you and that Spartanburg boy, despite warnings from dubious neighbors of your youth, are going on your twentieth year of wedded bliss, and still, somehow, reside in the upcountry, and you are happy there. Your parents in all their wisdom send their four adult children into a room with a list of their assets and say before shutting the door behind them, "Y'all figure it out, and let us know what you decide. We're going fishing."

When the figuring is done, your siblings have decided you should have Mama and Daddy's house when the time comes.

You don't want the time to come. Ever.

But you know that your happiest place on earth is there beside the river, that *that place* is your sacred place, the place where you are most connected to nature, your ancestors, and God, there among live oaks, salt breeze, exuberant mullet, and the primordial smells of the river. You know that just being there heals hurts of all kinds.

You are forty-four, and you've published a few stories and once even a novel. You're asked to write an essay about your favorite place in South Carolina. You nod. Yes. You can do that. Yours is a place that flows in your soul like lifeblood, its ebbing and flooding the rhythm of your being. In your mind's eye you see lowcountry rivers as sharp as a million shards of glass in sunshine, and you know exactly what you'll write. ☽

)

Willtown

I'd always wanted to live close to a big river, and in the early 1970s, I got my chance when my first husband and I rented a house at Willtown, an old rice plantation on the Edisto River twenty miles from the coast. The rent was cheap—$50 a month—because the owner and his family came out on weekends and he wanted tenants to keep an eye on the place when they weren't there. We lived at Willtown just long enough for me to fall in love with the place. Like any love, it's complicated, but more about that later.

First, a brief history. The earliest mention of the high ground above the Edisto appears in instructions from the Lords Proprietors to the Surveyor General in 1682. The name of the place shows up in 1697, and for the first half of the eighteenth century Willtown (or New London, the name of the town on the bluff above the river) was an important landmark on the Carolina frontier.

Rice was introduced into the colony around 1695, and by the end of the colonial period, the swamps around Willtown, and other riverfront plantations on a narrow strip of land that stretched from the Savannah to the Pee Dee Rivers, had become prime rice-producing real estate. This complex agricultural feat was accomplished by an intricate system of dams, gates, ditches, canals, and tidal changes to irrigate and drain fields at different times in the plant's growth cycle, and so the key to the success of a rice plantation was its location: far enough upriver to be above the incursion of salt water but close enough to the ocean for the river to rise and fall with the tides.

This narrow strip of swamp land was known as the Rice Kingdom, and its kings made huge fortunes using slaves to move river water in and out of their rice fields. From the mid- 1760s to 1780, the enslaved population of

The house at Willtown.
Photograph by Walter Shockley.

the lowcountry almost doubled from fifty-two thousand to one hundred thousand, and the numbers kept growing until the Civil War put an end to tidal rice farming as a money-making venture.

We entered this long flow of time in the early 1970s, and my memories of Willtown still come in a rush of vivid sense impressions. The main house on the river bluff and the grove of ancient live oaks draped with Spanish moss—the site of the original town—that stretched between the big house and our own, the shape of rice fields sketched in the marshes, and of course, and always, the magnificent, black-water river and its tides and changes.

I remember the smell of water-soaked wood, of green plants and mud and wood smoke. Across the river to the west, the marshes stretched to the horizon, and the sun set into the marshes every day. I remember how the sunset light came low through the grasses and the changing color of those grasses from summer green to the tawny gold, brown, and red of autumn. I remember the rushing sound of the grasses in the wind, and the clear, fluting call of the red-winged blackbirds that clung to the swaying stalks. Egrets stalking the shoreline at low tide. The taste of tomatoes grown in that rich soil.

I remember the immensity of night there, the depth of its silence and how, in that silence, I imagined I could hear the river sweep past the bluff with a sound like wind. I remember the river glinting with sunlight, and the river at the moment just before the tide turned, when it lay motionless and clear, like a mirror. In one of those moments of glassy stillness, a school of dolphins came diving and leaping upstream. To this day that sight remains one of the most beautiful I've ever seen.

Other impressions linger, too, of the hostile and death-dealing aspects of the place. This is where the love story starts to get fraught, complicated. Our beloved Irish setter lost a leg to an unstoppable infection there. Mold crawled up cracks in the cups and dishes in the kitchen cupboards. We came home one night to find a twitching carpet of termites in every room of the house. Alligators lurked in the old rice field ditches, and when a dog waded in, dozens of eyes appeared above the water. Then there were the snakes. Enormous water moccasins and rattlers coiled under clumps of saw palmetto. Five-foot copperheads sunning themselves in the sandy road that led down to the river landing. Sometimes it seemed that you couldn't leave the house without running into a snake.

Even the river could be treacherous. At Willtown, the Edisto curves like a flexed bow into the land. From the bluff the river seems to glide by, slow as honey, but that stately pace is an illusion because a tidal river is the ocean's

The Edisto River along Willtown Bluff.
Photograph by Walter Shockley.

instrument; its power is the power of a planetary force confined to a narrow channel. Dive into it on the outgoing tide, as I did once—only once—and the current seizes and carries you downstream so insistently even an able swimmer has to swim hard to make it back to the dock.

And the climate itself, my God. It's been over forty years since I lived at Willtown, and still, any suffocating prison of a summer day when the heat and humidity hover around a hundred and the pale sky is stacked high with thunderheads takes me back there, and I wonder again why anyone would willingly live in such a climate, much less labor there, without an air-conditioned house to retreat to.

Memory, the Southern historian Fitzhugh Brundage suggests, is "an active and ongoing process of re-ordering the past." I find the idea heartening: the past is subject to change, more net than tomb. You can open the past, it says, let light and air into the tangled mess of history, discover new pieces and re-order them, set beauty next to cruelty and darkness, give everything a place, make a bigger story. My own reordering of Willtown's past has meant reaching back and filling in that remembered landscape with what I've learned since, peopling it with the men who got up from the pews of the Presbyterian church at Willtown one Sunday in September of 1739 and rode out to crush the Stono rebellion and line the King's Highway with the heads of rebel slaves. With the rice kings and with the hundreds of men and women who cleared the swamps and built the embankments, ditched the rice fields, planted and harvested the rice, and repaired breaches in the embankments, night or day, in any season or weather. Those who drowned or died of snakebite or pneumonia, dysentery or malaria, who might have carried buckets on a wooden yoke, like the one I saw in the Charleston Museum, its edges worn thin against a human neck. Those who labored and somehow did not lose heart, who foiled the system, who ran away and disappeared—who knows where?—or survived into freedom.

I go to Willtown whenever I can. I like to take off my shoes and walk into the Edisto and feel the water flow over my feet. I seem to need to take the people I love to the river too, as I'm doing in a photograph of me and my toddler son standing ankle deep in the water. I love Willtown for the changes of heart, mind, and memory it has fostered and asked of me, for the river of lives that flowed through that place, and for the river itself, constant and ever changing. ♪

Women of Many Faiths, Columbia, June 2014.
Photo by Tracy Fredrychowski.

Coming Together

In 2002 four women of different faiths gathered in Columbia to learn about each other's beliefs. By 2014 Women of Many Faiths had close to one hundred members. Meeting monthly to discuss a range of topics, WOMF includes Baháʼís, Buddhists, Catholics, Hindus, Jews, Mormons, Muslims, Native Americans, Pagans, Protestants, Southern Baptists, Unitarians, and those in twelve-step programs.

"We value a diversity of backgrounds and perspectives and the opportunity to learn from one another in a spirit of openness, sensitivity, respect, trust, friendship and support" reads part of the group's Statement of Purpose.

Or, as member Ethel Crawford said when convening the June 2014 meeting, "different flowers in a garden—that's a good thing."

Susan Millar Williams

)

The Corner of Columbus and America

For almost twenty years now, I have worked at the corner of Columbus and America Streets, on the upper edge of downtown Charleston. Columbus and America: the heart of the East Side, formerly known as Hampstead. Columbus and America: the intersection of discovery and opportunity.

Looking back I feel like the stoic, self-sufficient Amelia Evans in Carson McCullers's *The Ballad of the Sad Café,* falling madly, helplessly in love with a hunchbacked dwarf. When I moved to South Carolina in 1986, "normal" people adored the Battery, the Miles Brewton House, Rainbow Row—the manicured, safe, romantic haunts of a city that liked to gaze at itself in the mirror. In the 1980s the East Side—a section of the Charleston peninsula east of Meeting Street and north of Calhoun, bordered by the bustling waterfront and the on-ramps to the Cooper River bridges—was famous mostly for crumbling houses, drug deals, and murders. If you found yourself driving through it, you made certain the car doors were locked. My new friends Martha Zierden and Dale Rosengarten were working on a history of the neighborhood, which would eventually be published as *Between the Tracks.* I thought they were very smart—and very brave.

In 1995 I took a job teaching English at Trident Technical College and landed full time at the Palmer Campus, named for a defunct business college and located in a former high school at the corner of Columbus and America. Every morning I drove into the parking lot and inhaled the delicious tang of onions frying at Johnson and Wales, a culinary school housed in the former factory building across the street. But like most of my colleagues, I rarely ventured beyond the fence that surrounded the campus. Once in a while I had to park outside the gates, and I was often warned that my car would be stripped when I got back. It never was. People who taught at Trident's Main Campus in North Charleston spoke of Palmer as Siberia, a place where you did hard time. But it grew on me.

In 2001 I started doing research for a book about Charleston's great earthquake with my coauthor Steve Hoffius. When the earthquake hit more than a century before, in 1886, the factory had just been built as a textile mill. It was promoted as a beacon of hope, a source of jobs, a hive of purposeful activity. The Almshouse, across the street, embodied despair. It was where Charlestonians ended up when they were destitute and didn't have families who could take them in. And by then the neighborhood already had a long and complicated history.

Henry Laurens, a signer of the Constitution, laid out Hampstead in 1769 as an upscale suburb modeled on an English village. Less than a dozen years later, a battle of the American Revolution raged nearby, drastically reducing the appeal of Laurens's residential lots. Starting in 1817, Denmark Vesey, a free black man, worshipped a few blocks south, plotting rebellion —or perhaps not—behind the sheltering walls of the African Church. During the Civil War, Charlestonians who lived south of Broad moved up into Hampstead to get away from the Union bombardment.

At the end of Reconstruction, when African Americans were pushed out of other city parks, Hampstead Mall became a place where black people could gather unmolested: they went there to rally, to talk politics, to celebrate Emancipation Day. On the Fourth of July, the park filled with food vendors and picnickers, kicking up their heels as they performed an African-inspired dance called the "Too-la-loo."

The Almshouse was long gone by the time I first saw Hampstead, replaced by an elementary school. But the factory and the park were still there, and so were a lot of beautiful houses, slumping and peeling. Just behind Palmer were the modest home and forge of Philip Simmons, the world-renowned blacksmith. There was a sense that Hampstead was the city's attic, that every building was an antique trunk concealing scraps of the past. Like downtown Charleston much earlier in the twentieth century, the neighborhood was experiencing a form of preservation by neglect.

When Steve and I finally finished *Upheaval in Charleston*, I started studying Hampstead in earnest. I began by walking the streets right around the campus. That sounds simple enough, but I had never done it. There were, at certain times of the day, lots of people on the streets. We nodded at each other, quickly averting our eyes. Each time I penetrated a few blocks farther my heart began to pound. I started noticing details—graffiti, gardens, elaborate moldings, the silent man who picked up trash with his dustpan-on-a-stick. I liked uncovering the secrets of Hampstead: tracking down remnants of the old mill village, learning that the beautiful Art Deco building now used as a community center had been built as the city incinerator, discovering that Booker T. Washington once visited the cotton factory.

And as I wandered the neighborhood, what I knew about Hampstead in the 1880s played in my head like the HBO series *Tremé.* I imagined the streets on a summer morning, the sky over the broad expanse of the Cooper River just turning pink. I saw the bricklayers go on strike for higher wages and shorter hours. I saw the walls of the factory rise until there were five bulky stories and a smokestack looming between Hampstead Mall and the water. I heard the city fathers talk up the factory as a source of respectable

Alice Flowers tending her flowers. Photograph by Margaret Wood Atwood.

Richard Nelson demonstrating the neighborly art of stoop sitting. Photograph by Margaret Wood Atwood.

work, and I saw hundreds of white women find employment there. I saw them learn to operate the complicated machines, powered by a titanic steam engine. The investors were sure the women would be grateful and help the factory turn a profit. Instead they quickly learned to hate their work. Crowds of unemployed men harassed them as they walked to and from their jobs. The hours were long, the pace relentless. Lint clouded the air and filled their lungs. The noise was deafening. Very few of the workers stayed on the job for long. In my mind's eye I watched the cotton factory fail, revive, hire black workers, and fail again.

Half a century later, the building was one of the largest cigar factories in the world. Many of the employees then were black women, segregated from their white counterparts. They operated a different set of complicated machines that churned out Roi-Tans and Cremos. In 1945, the tobacco workers union went on strike for higher wages and better conditions. And as the picket line stretched down Columbus Street, week after week, strikers trying to keep up their spirits began singing the beloved spiritual "I Shall Overcome." They changed the words slightly, to "We Shall Overcome." And in that moment, one short block from the corner of Columbus and America, the anthem of the civil rights movement was born.

The Palmer Campus, my home base, is housed in a historic building that is itself a relic of segregation. For years I dismissed C. A. Brown High School as a million-dollar hush-puppy, cooked up by the Charleston County School District to stave off integration. And then I started talking to my colleague Mary Edwards, a graduate of C. A. Brown. Mary told me

The author and Mary Edwards at the corner of Columbus and America. Photograph by Margaret Wood Atwood.

the other side of the story. She and her classmates adored their brand-new school, so bright and full of promise. They mourned when it was shuttered just twenty years after it opened.

Mary grew up on the East Side and now lives just two blocks from the campus. Soon she was taking me out for walks and introducing me to her friends. I still had a tendency to lurk, but Mary greeted her neighbors with a smile. They smiled back.

In Mary's world, people sit on their front stoops and kids play basketball in the park. Alice Flowers tends one patch of flowers that brighten the sidewalk by her house and another at Our Lady of Mercy Catholic Church, where hungry people stand in line for meals provided by the Neighborhood House. A tiny sweetshop sells honey buns and ice cream bars to children who tumble off the school bus. A small metal plaque marks the grave of a beloved dog named Romeo. Hannibal's Kitchen dishes up oxtails and shark steak.

In early 2014 the Hampstead neighborhood is just what it has always been: a place where hope and despair, industry and idleness, good and evil, mingle. It is not buffed and polished, preserved and cherished, catalogued and studied. Not yet. During a recent murder trial, a witness testified that when he Googled "Where can I buy heroin in Charleston?" the answer came back: "America Street."

Mary and I now lead tours of the neighborhood at least once a semester, and the people who live there come along to share their own stories.

The Palmer Campus, under the leadership of a dynamic college president, Dr. Mary Thornley, and a visionary campus dean, Dr. Louester Robinson, is state of the art, complete with a showpiece restaurant run by students. A five-year campaign to connect with the neighborhood culminated last November with an East Side Thanksgiving dinner. Before we had always held a potluck for ourselves—Palmer faculty and staff. It was nice, low-key, and we looked forward from year to year to Larry's pickled shrimp, Kathy's collards, and other home-cooked treats. But in 2013, the time seemed right to expand Palmer's sense of community. We started by inviting all the people who depend on the Neighborhood House for food and clothing. Students volunteered to serve them, faculty and staff donated food. Our guests arrived in a steady stream, first the Neighborhood House regulars, and then, as the word spread, couples with young children, elderly women, construction workers, even, as one of my wide-eyed students pointed out, at least one notorious drug dealer. Everyone was gracious, mannerly, thankful—and the food miraculously held out until all comers were fed.

Today decrepit houses are being renovated at a rate that boggles the mind. The upper reaches of nearby King and Meeting Streets are turning into the cool part of town, full of upscale restaurants and bars and funky retail establishments. The Cigar Factory is about to be reinhabited, starting with a fancy grocery and "culinary complex." Hampstead will soon be the filling in a high-stakes development sandwich.

Okay, so maybe I'm not really Miss Amelia Evans with an unlikely crush on my strange, twisted cousin. Maybe I'm more like Davis on *Tremé*, whose passion for the music of a down-and-out New Orleans neighborhood eventually leads him to give walking tours that look an awful lot like mine: a bunch of well-dressed people gawking at rundown buildings. Loudmouthed and annoying as he is, Davis understands that it's the stories that matter, that make people care.

Will Hampstead still make my heart beat faster when it's all spiffed up? Will the current residents of the East Side find ways to stay and share in its transformation? I hope so. Hampstead has been a neighborhood in transition ever since Henry Laurens first carved it out of the marsh in the late eighteenth century. Soldiers fought and died there. Businesses and industries thrived—until they didn't. Ethnic groups moved in—and moved out. Discovering Hampstead's history is like stripping the paint from a historic building, one thin layer at a time. Every flake of paint is an important clue to a stage in the structure's evolution. And perhaps when all is said and done, Hampstead's breathtaking ability to adapt is the quality I love most. ☽

Emily L. Cooper

Music from the Porch

I love being immersed in memories painted onto our wide front porch—sitting in the swing and savoring that huge oak, reminding me of sitting on the late Eulalie Salley's porch in Aiken as she pointed out her live oak's resurrection fern after a summer rain. Or remembering Mother and Daddy sitting on our porch in the slant of the September sun and having iced tea. Or seeing the joggling board Wiley Cooper bought for our tenth anniversary, where grandchildren bounced and big people became kids again.

I have been happiest when that porch has been in full clatter, gaggles of women or clusters of Sunday school friends pouring wine at my grandmother's marble table on the far side of the wraparound porch.

College Place's churchwomen traditionally gathered on its front steps for a picture at their annual spring meeting. Then there was the day the block party was held in front of our house and a little shower drove them onto this wonderful porch. The porch—and the whole house—had been spit-polished when the Columbia Board of Realtors was invited to meet here with school and community leaders in a neighborhood they once openly shunned in defiance of fair housing law.

I greeted the bishop and his wife when they came up these steps; Wiley had taken them and the staff of the South Carolina United Methodist Conference Center on a tour of this large community. Most had been locked in that center more than a decade, afraid of "bogeymen," despite our Methodist church across the street staying unlocked and unharmed twelve or more hours a day.

You see, this house sits in the middle of a majority-black neighborhood. We, as whites, are the minority.

The old live oak welcomes a new occupant being backed in and set on new pillars. Photograph courtesy of the author.

It hadn't always been so. College Place—one of Columbia's earliest "suburbs"—is one of twenty-six neighborhoods in Eau Claire. Eau Claire was once an all-white, incorporated town on the northeast side of Columbia.

In fact, this house hasn't always been here. It was a block down the street.

In 1995, Wiley was coming to be the new pastor to College Place United Methodist, a church that had already crossed a few barriers, including race and gender identification, and continued as a diverse and positive center of the community. Realtors declined to show us houses in Eau Claire—they "wouldn't feel safe"—so we were looking around. When we heard the late Niven Cantwell's house was to be demolished to build a parking lot next to Shives Funeral Home, we visited the funeral director. "I'll give it to you if you'll move it," he quickly responded.

We had redone three houses, one just eleven feet wide. "Piece of cake! We'll take it!" We hadn't fully realized the difference in size and work; this house was thirty-six feet wide!

With the confidence of children in the talents of J. E. Oswalt and Sons House Movers, we watched as this giant mobile home—porch and all—came down Colonial Drive and was backed onto its new foundation.

Our church members soon filled the yard for a house blessing. Punch was served in a dining room devoid of plaster.

It was clear some contractors were uneasy working in "dangerous Eau Claire" so I didn't want them either. I became the general contractor, figuring any time I had three trucks lined up alongside the port-a-john I was making real progress. The house stood open for more than two months during the renovations and not even a hammer was stolen.

Nick Pizzuti started building a new kitchen and bath on the back, and Preston Wilson used his carpentry talents on the original house, building the wide porch steps that insinuated Old South gentility.

Our "new" home began its first life in 1910. Lumber dealer Thomas McGill built it when his daughter Niven was fourteen. Columbia College, a pre–Civil War women's college, had moved to the community six years before. The trolley that served the school came up the center of Colonial Drive, past the McGill place. McGill and his wife, Rebecca, stalwarts of College Place Church, had a large downstairs bedroom with a rose bush planted outside their window; their daughters, son, and a sister-in-law slept in the four bedrooms upstairs. When Niven married John Cantwell, an upstairs bath was added, and they shared her bedroom, the one she would occupy until her death.

This same house entertained soldiers from Fort Jackson on Sundays and heard the tinkle of fine china in the dining room when Columbia College faculty and staff were invited.

We know Niven only by her teasing, allowing the hall light to burn just when she chooses. I rub my hand over the cannonball newel post and think how many times she did the same in the eighty-four years she lived here.

Today's visitor may think life here picture-perfect, but it hasn't always been so. In fact, we find the neighborhood to be pretty dull these days. We seldom hear police cars flying up our four-lane street. I can sit in the double front-parlors and read undisturbed, having long given up the unrealistic worry of a drive-by shooter.

A family of drug dealers once lived a few doors down and had been dealing across from Arden school for fifteen years. Wiley was working on the side-porch door one afternoon when the family's two brothers ran up on the porch, yelling, "Call the police! She shot me!" A woman drove into our driveway. I was already dialing 911. "Let us in!" they demanded. Wiley refused, told them to wait on the porch and led our barking dog toward the woman's car—who by that time was letting go of words you don't always hear at a preacher's house.

"If you don't get out of here, I'm going to let this dog loose," Wiley warned. She got in her car and backed away. The men were still insisting on getting inside; Wiley, equally insistent, walked them back to their house to wait for the police and an ambulance. "Guess where she shot him?" Wiley said when he returned. "A few inches below his crotch."

With company in the house one night, we slept in the front room and heard drug customers' constant foot traffic. Exhausted, I wrote an "I'm-mad-as-hell" letter to the police chief and mayor, and surprise: after years of "trying" to bust the dealers, they did it. One dealer went to prison and the family moved to the country, but not before a woman living there showed up about 2 A.M. with plenty of bruises while she waited for the police. This house had become a "safe house."

All sorts of nefarious things went on at a dwelling known as the "pink house." Another young dealer brazenly met his clients in front of his home.

Now older and younger African Americans have blended with Euro-Americans, some who heroically dug in their heels during the 1970s down-town "urban renewal" era when Realtors knocked on Eau Claire doors to say, "I sold the house next door to a black couple. Wouldn't you like to list your house?" It became a neighborhood of strength built on adversity.

Colonial Drive is as quiet as any city street, quieter than some, with little to get the adrenalin going as we look out our wide Craftsman windows. But the house is always eager for a party. Thus it seemed appropriate to celebrate President Obama's 2008 election, a black man elected to lead this diverse and yet historically prejudiced nation.

Candles glowed. This old house was alive with exultations. More than a dozen people stood in one of the parlors, holding hands and sharing what the night before had meant. A few tears choked our voices.

Judy was reminded of being in the crowd the day Nelson Mandela was released from prison in South Africa. That night we all were releasing a deeply held breath of air.

Bettie had thought of her first day at a formerly all-black school in Greenville. On the outside it was one of Governor Byrnes's "separate-but-equal" schools, similar to white schools she knew; but on the inside, there were vast differences. Classrooms had an exposed tin roof and no cross ven-tilation. Unsanded wooden desks tore kids' clothes and were topped with different colors of leftover laminate.

An unprompted vision had popped into my head election night—lynched black men who had risen to dance around a bonfire on Edgefield's town square, the place I had learned about prejudice and awful injustices.

Former state leader Milton Kimpson shared his memories: playing with the white boy where his mother was the domestic and his family the sharecroppers. The little boys would see the school bus go by and talk about what fun they were going to have together when they got on that bus and went to school. Of course, Milt said, when they turned six, the white boy got on the bus and went to school. He walked almost four miles to the "colored school."

Tears give a house depth. Memories give it music. Love gives it all that matters. Someday, maybe all the new owners will know of the Coopers will be from a glimpse of a couple dancing in the dining room. ☽

The Park with No Past

When I was young, it was cemeteries.

Back then, St. Philip's graveyard was the most alluring, offering an escape from my adolescent angst and unarticulated longings. In college, between classes, I sought refuge in Second Presbyterian's churchyard at Meeting and Charlotte Streets. High and aloof, it had an almost bucolic feel, while densely silent St. Philip's, surrounded by the bustling city, was more allegorical, like a moral to a story.

Finding a bench or a place under a tree, I'd sit and read melancholy poems —"Lines above Tintern Abbey," "Dover Beach," or Gray's "Elegy." The prose I chose was by Hawthorne, Melville, or Faulkner. I favored writers obsessed with the big questions of life and death, the line between, and the compulsion to find meaning.

Why angels and obelisks, urns, hour glasses with wings, and other symbols of death were so comforting, I don't know. Maybe they possessed that which I lacked and yearned for—a simple answer to the quandaries and complexities of life I was then on the verge of entering. The places were lovely: the tombstones' hues varying from gray to lilac, the trailing moss with sun streaking through green leaves, the stained and veined statuary. There were very few burials, no real death or trauma, and the rawness of red earth and yawning holes gaping open like the mouth in Munch's *The Scream* appeared rarely. So the places spoke not so much of grief as of peace. If someone wandered by, I'd hope to be overlooked or mistaken for a piece of statuary.

Eventually, I was compelled to leave the dead; I graduated college and had to make a living. In the historical society where I worked, I became familiar with the history of the city. That way, I got to know their denizens and so evolved a different take on cemeteries.

Of course, this being Charleston, there were the names recycled from tombstones to those (temporarily) living. But something different happened the day I came upon a tombstone of a man whose Civil War diary I had held in my hands just that morning; an electric shock galvanized me. *Why, I know you,* I could say more and more often to those whose epitaphs I bent down to read.

With new knowledge filling the gaps between birth and death dates, the stones began to speak: *Spoon River* was now my analogy. One hot June day, I stole into St. Philip's graveyard, opened a small blue book and read DuBose Heyward's "Epitaph for a Poet" standing on DuBose Heyward's grave on his death's anniversary.

Looming a few yards away was the tomb of John C. Calhoun. I not only knew what Calhoun looked like (deep crazed eyes, dramatic gestures, and even more dramatic hair) but was familiar with his beliefs. His devotion to the inequality of humans and his rabid support of slavery had helped split the nation and send hundreds of thousands of young men to take up their postures of eternity. Yet in Charleston he had a place of honor. I avoided his tombstone like you might a creep at a party.

So oddly, now that I knew the lives of their occupants, the cemeteries began to spook me. And the ghosts of the past followed me out into the streets. I felt the heavy presence of the dead everywhere now, dense and debilitating as the humidity.

The delicate and fragile beauty of Charleston, I began to suspect, was a façade, hiding a violent past marred by the moral corruption and cruelty of slavery, in just the same way mellowed indecipherable tombstones dissembled the pangs of life and the agony of dying. The place was gorgeous, but what price beauty? The whole city seemed a perfect example of Hawthorne's story "Rappaccini's Daughter," wherein a lovely woman raised in a lush garden of poisons exhales deadly fumes. My lovely hometown did too, killing the possibility of a new social order rising. Old ideals of status and birth, coupled with indifference to its sinful past, paralyzed the place. To speak this truth was considered rude, tantamount to desecrating a shrine or being ugly to a gentle old lady.

Sometimes these thoughts made me feel disloyal, and I longed for the simpler view, the benign and uncomplicated way of seeing things. I wanted to close my eyes, lie in the sun, and fall back in that drugged and lulled half-awake half-asleep state that triggers dreams, not doubts. A social conscience was intruding upon my love of the old city.

I escaped my inner civil war when life took me away from Charleston. I returned a decade later, wary as around an old lover or dangerous associates no good for you. I vowed I'd never let the city again trap and seduce me.

But its languor, its indifference, its shameless gorgeousness was overwhelming.

When I needed a place to retreat for consolation or peace, graveyards would not do. John C. Calhoun frowned down on me in Marion Square. The Confederate dead were pointedly present in their obelisk in Washington Park, and White Point Garden lionized the Confederate defenders of Fort Sumter and the city.

I found myself going more and more to the new Waterfront Park on the Cooper River, built in my absence. The park faced east, allowing you to literally turn your back on Charleston. Walking along the railings, or hanging over them to peer into the rich alluvial life of the marsh, you could pretend

Children play in Charleston's welcoming pineapple fountain.
Photograph by Katie West.

you were on an ocean liner, sliding out to sea. There were walkways, views falling into place, garden rooms opening up like origami, wharfs and walks into the harbor, alleyways lined with arching trees, and water reverberating everywhere, from tidal urges at the shore to the cascading pineapple fountain within.

It was always busy, but never crowded. And everyone seemed happy—tourists, people with dogs, dogs with Frisbees, old folks walking, and half-naked children in the fountains, giddily screaming. Limousines would draw up on the stone street to let out brides and grooms in white gowns and black tie to be photographed. Other, more colorful parties exploded into the park too—voluble excited groups of men, women and children of various ethnic groups, languages, and nationalities, often in saris or bright primary colors to shame Rainbow Row's oh-so-tasteful hues.

There was a new tableau every time I looked up: kids in droopy drawers, skateboarders, palmetto rose sellers, lonely souls eager to catch your eye and engage you. Those sitting formally on the stiff ornate benches or sprawled informally sunning themselves on lawns all seemed at home, as if this park were theirs, and they were happily entertaining.

Eventually it hit me what was so special about the place and why everyone felt at ease: the past had not gotten a toehold yet; there was no one else's history here.

The park's designers had designed wisely. Only bases had been built. Yes, the park had pedestals, but as if they had gone off for a smoking break, no statues. There were no bronze heroes with feet of clay and sightless eyes to look down on us. (Folks in the future would be burdened with whom to honor here.) With no one enthroned, we could roam free with no lessons to learn or looming supersized statues to make us feel unworthy or puny.

Instead there were black and white kids, jumping up on those empty pedestals, striking dramatic poses crying *look at me, look at me,* as if they, the living, were the heroes of the city—not Calhoun, nor even Moultrie. Sometimes lovers whirled each other dizzily on the round daises like music box figurines.

We were all in a history-free zone untainted with memories of segregation, unfairness, or even irony. Nothing needed to be explained or avoided. You could breathe in without apologies, be in a moment innocent of allegories.

And so because of its views—and no doubt because of mine—because of its beauty, accessibility and democratic nature, it became my favorite spot in the city.

Waterfront Park still is, though lately a few monuments have crept in, and more are coming. The past is a thief sneaking in to steal the present, to transmute gold to lead, change a living moment to a dead memory. But know what? There's comfort in the fact that no matter what statues rise, no matter what words are carved for us to read, the park will always revolve around its central pineapple fountain dedicated not to a hero or heroine but to hospitality.

And so, even as it changes, Waterfront Park is where you'll find me, dreaming, observing, just *being* in this enticing intersection of land and sky and sea unplagued by the past, a park immersed more in the moment than in memento mori. ☽

Perched, brown pelican, acrylic on board by Becky Hyatt Rickenbaker.

Roosting

Nothing is more ridiculously dignified than a Brown Pelican perched atop a dock piling, beak on breast, giving the observer a most solemn stare.

Alexander Sprunt Jr. and E. Burnham Chamberlain,
South Carolina Bird Life, 1949

Island Time

Long ago we called this place "the island." We knew a dozen other sea islands nearby, but "the" island was Sullivan's, a three-mile strip of sand and
old beach houses running slantwise from the mouth of Charleston Harbor
northeastward. The slant was something we ignored. We all spoke as if the
island ran south to north, so the sun and moon rose in our north and set
in our south; the North Star appeared in our west. It was a sweet, magical,
innocent time and place. There was so much we didn't know.

The sweetness of memory is a gift of time and grows with time. Now
that I've spent sixty-eight summers on the island (and today live here year-
round), memory is even sweeter and stronger than reality. I walk the streets
and seem to see not the existing houses but those that used to be, with
sunbaked yards of brown grasses and cockleburs, oleanders and myrtles (the
island was too dry and sandy for much of anything else), and suddenly I'm
walking barefoot with my sisters and cousins down the tar-and-gravel road
to the Triangle Grocery Store, for Sugar Daddies and candy cigarettes and
maybe some wax lips. Back then we didn't know sugar was not such a good
idea. We walked home with our mouths full of sweetness and our feet picking up oozy warm tar and grit, past the weather-beaten houses with wide
screen porches and outside showers, the sounds of radios and children, the
smell of shrimp and tomatoes. At night we slept to the sound of the surf,
a whisper if the wind was from our west, a roar if from our east (but from
any direction it would sing in the screens). If we were lucky we might wake
up in the middle of the night and run to the window for a look at the
phantasmagorical night-machine that came spraying what we thought was
water for the oleanders and palmettos, not knowing it was DDT for the
mosquitoes.

The ideal observation station.
Photo illustration by Josephine Humphreys.

The house wasn't really ours but belonged to my father's favorite cousins, Aunt El and Uncle Ray, who always invited us to spend the summers with them. It was open and airy. Upstairs were two children's rooms, each with walls of unpainted pine, three white iron beds, a sink, and a dormer window. The dormer created a sort of tiny room, and I loved slipping into it to look out onto the wide flat beach and the Atlantic Ocean.

I was a born watcher, and the ocean drew me more than any other spectacle. At a glance it looked unchanging, a gray-blue field ruffling white along the shore. But if I waited, if I somehow lost the thought of myself, the action sped up. A long slow line of pelicans would suddenly spot fish invisible to me and in their frenzy drop headlong into the sea. A speck on the horizon morphed into a looming freighter; a thin cloud gathering in the east (actually the south) could balloon in an instant, and darken, and spawn a squall that cleared the beach of swimmers and sent sunbathers running. In the dormer I learned something of the nature of time and its surprises. Island time was different from clock time. More mysterious, more unpredictable.

For example, a summer was eternal until suddenly it was gone. Time stopped in June; in September it tore off again into the future. But in that interim, we children had time for everything under the sun—and we usually *were* under the sun. In the dunes we played days on end with the boy next door, who was clever and curly-haired, and in love with my sister. Down the road in one direction (we called it south) were the black concrete fortifications remaining from some war we could not name but thanked, for leaving us those winding corridors and cells to explore. In a different direction (our west) was another wartime remnant, one of several huge earthen bunkers that were the island's only hills. Inside it there was a hole said to be so deep that if you fell into it, no one would hear your cries, and you were in it forever. So we stuck to the hillside with cardboard boxes as sleds on the grassy slopes. Or we walked six blocks "north" to our grandfather's house, a dark green ramshackle cottage built from the wreckage of a ship that had foundered on the beach long ago. There was a possum trap under the house, a hammock on the sleeping porch, yellow jackets in the yard, and a joggling board next to the front door. Behind the house stood a tiny one-room dwelling for Isabel. Every summer she left her own family and stayed on the island with my grandparents, to do the ironing. I never went inside, in all those summers.

There was so much we didn't know.

Looking back I understand there were clues we half-noticed but paid no attention to, omens that hinted at possibilities we did not expect. From the dormer at night sometimes I saw the flashlight beams crossing back and forth across the surf. This happened every time someone drowned in the undertow, but I was safe up in my little lookout corner and didn't think much about it. When the curly-haired neighbor boy told me there was a hidden place on the island where thousands of slaves had been kept in a pen, I dismissed the idea because my parents said he had made it up. I was never afraid when the little hurricanes came through, even the night when all seven children had the measles and Uncle Ray and my father hammered together a buttress of two-by-fours to brace the wall against the wind. I always felt safe. I always felt innocent.

Today everything I have mentioned here is gone. The Triangle Grocery is no more. My grandparents are long dead, my parents recently so. A family rift that I still don't understand split us from our cousins. The boy who loved my sister was killed in a car wreck. Every splinter of Aunt El's house vanished when Hurricane Hugo brought the ocean sweeping across

Sullivan's Island, 2014.
Photograph courtesy of the author.

the island in 1989, and more than a hundred houses disappeared or were wrecked beyond repair.

The island recovered from Hugo but in ways that transformed it so radically I can't call it "the" island any more. It's green and shady with trees and landscaped yards and automatic irrigation systems. The enormous new houses have generators and air-conditioning and security systems. I don't hear music or children's hubbub coming from these sealed-up houses, only the sound of mechanical systems. But what surprises me is that in spite of the changes, I still love this place with all my heart. I know now that the boy's story was true: almost half of all the enslaved Africans brought into North America came through Sullivan's Island, where they were quarantined before being sold in the city. And still I love the place. Maybe I love it even more, for having a difficult complexity I didn't see back then, looking out from my dormer window, still young and marveling, my family intact, the ocean in its place, all temporarily eternal. ☽

Contributors

RON AIKEN still writes poetry that's just as unpublished now as ever but fortunately earns his living as a journalist. He has won numerous state and national awards for his writing and journalism and had a story anthologized in a university press featuring the year's best technology writing. In 2013 he won first-place awards from the South Carolina Press Association for best feature writing and sports writing and second place for best business writing. He lives in Columbia.

JACK BASS lives in Charleston, close enough to the Atlantic that he can still walk on the beach, with uncrowded Sullivan's Island his favorite. He grew up in the town of North in Orangeburg County and is the author or coauthor of nine books, one of them the winner of the Robert F. Kennedy Book Award. His most recent book is *The Palmetto State: The Making of Modern South Carolina*.

NANCY BROCK is the 2014 South Carolina Academy of Authors Fiction Fellowship winner and a six-time finalist in the Pirate's Alley Faulkner-Wisdom Literary Competition. Her prize-winning short story, "Davy Crockett's Last Stand," appeared in *Fall Lines: A Literary Convergence*. An active disaster volunteer with the American Red Cross, Brock worked in New Orleans after Hurricane Katrina and in New York after Hurricane Sandy. She lives in Columbia, where she serves on the South Carolina Book Festival Advisory Committee.

A native son of North Carolina's Great Smokies, **JIM CASADA** is a "recovering professor" (he taught history at Winthrop for twenty-five years) who took early retirement to become a full-time freelancer specializing in outdoor-related topics. Love of and closeness to the land has been a critical influence in all his work. He lives in Rock Hill, still spends considerable time in his highland homeland, and has long been a keen student of sporting scribes and noted conservationists from America's past. His major project at present is a biography of Archibald Rutledge, an iconic figure in sporting letters who was South Carolina's first poet laureate.

EMILY L. COOPER is a South Carolina newspaper reporter, editor, and publisher who went north for a stint as a congressional press secretary. She handled public affairs for national and South Carolina trade associations, and recently edited the *South Carolina United Methodist Advocate*. She is author of *Eulalie* and *Queen of the Lost*, stories of two women who lived in the same house thirty years apart.

RONALD DAISE, performing artist and writer, is the author of *Gullah Branches, West African Roots* and four other books. Costar and cultural consultant for *Gullah Gullah Island*, Nick Jr. TV's award-winning show of the 1990s, he is vice president for Creative Education at Brookgreen Gardens and the former chairman of the federal Gullah Geechee Cultural Heritage Corridor Commission. He and his wife Natalie live on Pawleys Island and are parents of three adult children, Sara and Simeon Daise and Sabrina Danielle Green.

CHRISTOPHER DICKEY is the author of six books, including *Summer of Deliverance: A Memoir of Father and Son*, which begins and ends at Pawleys Island. He is the foreign editor for the *Daily Beast*. He lives in Paris, New York, and on airplanes. His new book, *Our Man in Charleston: Britain's Secret Agent in the Civil War South*, is set in South Carolina at the time of Secession.

TIM DRIGGERS has written about popular music, sports, and food for various South Carolina publications. His humor column, the Fosnick Report, appeared for years in the *Lexington Dispatch-News* and the *Richland Northeast News Weekly*. He and Aïda Rogers are coauthors of *Stop Where the Parking Lot's Full*, a guidebook to South Carolina's favorite restaurants. He practices law in his native Lexington.

Former editor of *Lake Murray* and *Reach Out, Columbia* magazines in Columbia, SUE DUFFY (1948–2014) was also the published author of suspense novels. Her fifth, *Deeper Than Red*, the last of the Red Returning trilogy, was released in spring 2014. She lived, with her husband, Mike, on Lake Murray for fourteen years.

PAM DURBAN is the author of four books of fiction: a collection of short stories, *All Set About with Fever Trees*, and three novels, *The Laughing Place, So Far Back*, winner of the 2001 Lillian Smith Award for Fiction, and *The Tree of Forgetfulness*. Her fiction has been published in many magazines and anthologies, and her short story "Soon" was anthologized in *The Best American Short Stories of the Century*, edited by John Updike. A new collection of short stories was published in spring 2015 by Story River Books. Born in Aiken, Durban teaches at the University of

North Carolina in Chapel Hill, where she is the Doris Betts Distinguished Professor of Creative Writing.

MARGARET SHINN EVANS is the publisher and editor of *Lowcountry Weekly,* where she's been provoking readers with her regular Rants and Raves column since 1999. Her articles and essays have appeared in various publications throughout the Southeast, most recently in the new book *South: Essays and Images.* She is the former editor of *Beaufort Magazine* and enjoys a rollicking side gig as editorial assistant to Pat Conroy. Margaret lives in Beaufort with her husband, Jeff, their daughter, Amelia, and their two cats, Arthur and Frodo.

HERB FRAZIER grew up in the Ansonborough public housing projects in Charleston and at the U.S. Naval Base at Guantanamo Bay, Cuba. He has edited and reported for five daily newspapers, including his hometown paper, the *Post and Courier,* and was named Journalist of the Year in 1990 by the South Carolina Press Association. Frazier taught newswriting as a visiting lecturer at Rhodes University in South Africa and is a former Michigan Journalism Fellow at the University of Michigan. He is the author of *Behind God's Back,* and his next book, *Crossing the Sea on a Sacred Song,* tells the story of an ancient African funeral song that links Mary Moran of coastal Georgia with Baindu Jabati of Sierra Leone. Frazier is the public relations and marketing manager for Magnolia Plantation and Gardens in Charleston.

SAMMY FRETWELL is a South Carolina native whose ancestors moved to Anderson County in the early 1800s. He has been a journalist for thirty years, working at newspapers in Myrtle Beach; Columbia; and Montgomery, Alabama. He covers the environment beat for the *State* newspaper. He is a Columbia resident and University of South Carolina journalism school graduate.

SHANI GILCHRIST is a freelance journalist in Columbia whose work has appeared in *Free Times, Columbia Metropolitan Magazine,* DiscoverSouthCarolina.com, *The Equals,* volume 1, and more. She is still puzzling out a plan to live at least part-time in lower Richland County.

VERA GÓMEZ, who was born in Texas and has lived in Greenville since 1993, firmly believes in the power of words. She is a performance poet, writer, and workshop facilitator whose collection of poems, *Barrios Voices,* was published in 2008. Her short story "A Dry Run," was a South Carolina Fiction Project winner (2006), and her work has appeared in *Yemassee* (2009), *KaKaLak: Anthology of Carolina Poets* (2006), *Millennial Sampler/South Carolina Poetry Anthology* (2005), *Ties That Bind* (2003), and *Quintet* (2003). Vera also is a teaching poet through Greenville's

SmartArts program and works as a writer/pursuit strategist in business sales, marketing, and communications.

A native of the city he writes about, **HARLAN GREENE** is an award-winning novelist and archivist. He is head of Special Collections of Addlestone Library at the College of Charleston.

RACHEL HAYNIE is the author of *First, You Explore: The Story of the Young Charles Townes*, released in 2014 by the University of South Carolina Press. Earlier releases include *Myths and Mysteries of South Carolina* and *Cornfield to Airfield: A History of Columbia Army Air Base*. A USC graduate, she frequently writes about art and history.

TOMMY HAYS'S first middle-grade novel, *What I Came to Tell You*, was chosen as a fall 2013 Okra Pick by the Southern Independent Booksellers Alliance (SIBA). His novel, *The Pleasure Was Mine*, was a Finalist for the SIBA Fiction Award and has been chosen for numerous community reads. His other novels are *In the Family Way* and *Sam's Crossing*. He directs the Great Smokies Writing Program and is Core Faculty for the Master of Liberal Arts program at UNC Asheville.

JOSEPHINE HUMPHREYS, a native of Charleston, is the award-winning author of four novels, *Dreams of Sleep, Rich in Love, The Fireman's Fair,* and *Nowhere Else on Earth*. She graduated from Duke University, where she studied writing with Reynolds Price. A member of the South Carolina Academy of Authors and the Fellowship of Southern Writers, she lives on Sullivan's Island with her husband, Tom Hutcheson, and their dog, Archie.

Son of a career U.S. Navy chaplain and an Alabama-born mother with eighteenth-century South Carolina roots, **THOMAS L. JOHNSON** is a retired librarian emeritus from the University of South Carolina (South Caroliniana Library) in Columbia, where he also taught English. He has been publishing prize-winning poetry since the 1970s and has received awards for both his short fiction and his work as an editor. His 1986 book, *A True Likeness,* won a Lillian Smith Award from the Southern Regional Council. In 2010 Ninety-Six Press of Greenville published *The Costume: New and Selected Poems* by Johnson. From 2003 until 2014 Johnson lived in Spartanburg, where he was active in the Hub City Writers Project, the Spartanburg Art Museum, and the Birchwood Center for Arts and Folklife in Pickens County. A life member of the board of governors of the South Carolina Academy of Authors, Johnson moved to Asheville, North Carolina, at the end of 2014.

CHARLES JOYNER is Burroughs Distinguished Professor Emeritus of Southern History and Culture at Coastal Carolina University. Best-known for his prize-winning *Down by the Riverside,* which was cited as "the finest work ever written on American slavery," Joyner also wrote *Shared Traditions* and other books. He holds two earned doctorates and taught at the University of California Berkeley, Ole Miss, and the University of Sydney, Australia. A fellow of the South Carolina Academy of Authors and the Society of American Historians, Joyner served as president of the Southern Historical Association in 2004–5. He lives in his native Myrtle Beach.

JANNA MCMAHAN is the national best-selling author of the novels *Anonymity, Calling Home,* and *The Ocean Inside.* She has received a number of literary awards including being named a finalist for the Flannery O'Connor Award. She was recently selected Literary Artist of the Year by readers of *Jasper Magazine.* Her website is www.JannaMcMahan.com. She lives in Columbia.

RAY MCMANUS is the author of three books of poetry: *Driving through the Country before You Are Born* (USC Press, 2007), *Red Dirt Jesus* (Marick Press, 2011), and *Punch* (Hub City Press, 2014). He is a professor of English at the University of South Carolina Sumter, where he teaches Southern literature, Irish literature, and creative writing. Ray grew up on a dirt road in Lexington County, and when he comes back to visit his parents, he does his best to drive slowly and dodge the ruts.

BEN MCC. MOÏSE is a retired conservation officer with the South Carolina Department of Natural Resources. He is a freelance writer and author of *Ramblings of a Lowcountry Game Warden: A Memoir,* and editor of *A Southern Sportsman: The Hunting Memoirs of Henry Edwards Davis.* He lives in downtown Charleston with his wife, Anne, and their Boykin, Belle III.

MARY ALICE MONROE is the *New York Times, USA Today* best-selling author of many highly acclaimed novels. Recipient of the South Carolina Center for the Book Award and South Carolina Literary Excellence Award, Monroe is an active conservationist who lives in the South Carolina lowcountry.

University of South Carolina First Lady PATRICIA MOORE-PASTIDES is the author of two award-winning books about the benefits of the traditional Mediterranean diet. Royalties from *Greek Revival: Cooking for Life,* and *Greek Revival: Growing and Cooking for Life,* have been invested in vegetable gardens on USC campuses statewide. By encouraging students, faculty, and staff to gain gardening experience and identify community partners to help them grow their own vegetables, Moore-Pastides is helping combat food deserts in South Carolina. The author has a master's degree in public health from Yale University and focuses on exercise, nutrition, and wellness.

GLENIS REDMOND is poet in residence at the Peace Center for the Performing Arts in Greenville, South Carolina, and the State Theatre in New Brunswick, New

Jersey. Dubbed the "Road Warrior Poet," she travels the country more than seven months each year teaching and performing poetry. When off the road, she considers herself Bi-Carolinian, biding her time between Greenville, South Carolina, and Charlotte, North Carolina. Her latest work, *The Joint: What the Body Holds,* addresses her challenges of living with fibromyalgia, while still embracing her first love, dance.

Retired educator and humorist **ROSE ROCK** volunteers for various youth programs through the South Carolina Department of Juvenile Justice. Mother of ten, seven of whom she birthed, Rock is the author of *Mama Rock's Rules: Ten Lessons for Raising a Houseful of Successful Children.* Her honors include Pajama Program Mother of the Year and the Dr. M. A. Lee Foundation's Living Legacy Award. Her new book, *Still Ruling,* focuses on the complexities of rearing older children. The national spokesperson for the Head Start alumni, Rock is an Andrews native who lives in Georgetown.

AÏDA ROGERS is a writer and editor in Columbia and McClellanville whose feature journalism has won regional and national awards. Except for three years in Georgia, she has lived and worked in the Palmetto State, currently at the South Carolina Honors College at her alma mater, the University of South Carolina.

Beaufort native **VALERIE SAYERS** is a professor of English at the University of Notre Dame. She has published six novels, and her stories, essays, and reviews appear widely. Her literary honors include a National Endowment for the Arts literature fellowship and a Pushcart Prize for fiction.

Born, bred, and Bar Mitzvah-ed in Beaufort, **BERNIE SCHEIN** plans to be buried (naturally, in the Jewish Cemetery) in his hometown. He's been featured and published in *Atlanta Magazine,* the *Atlanta Journal-Constitution, Newsweek, Creative Loafing,* and other magazines, journals, and periodicals. His most recent book prior to *Famous All Over Town* (2014) is *If Holden Caulfield Were in My Classroom.* His first book (coauthored with his wife, Martha Schein), *Open Classrooms in Middle School,* was a featured selection of the Educators' Book Club. A graduate of Newberry College with a master's degree in education from Harvard University, Bernie writes, speaks, and tells stories about his life as a Jewish southerner. An educator for forty-five years, he is also an educational consultant, doing workshops, giving talks, and telling stories about the kids in his classroom at the Paideia School in Atlanta, where, after serving as principal of three different schools, he taught for thirty-three years. Married to the psychologist Dr. Martha Schein, Bernie has two daughters—the writer and philosopher Dr. Maggie Schein and the teacher Lara Alexander Williams—and two granddaughters, Sofie and Caitlin. He lives in Beaufort.

GEORGE SINGLETON has published six collections of stories—*These People Are Us, The Half-Mammals of Dixie, Why Dogs Chase Cars, Drowning in Gruel, Stray Decorum,* and *Between Wrecks.* His two novels are *Novel* and *Work Shirts for Madmen,* and his one book of writing advice is *Pep Talks, Warnings, and Screeds.* Singleton's short stories have appeared in the *Atlantic Monthly, Harper's, Book, Playboy, Agni, Zoetrope, Georgia Review, Southern Review, Five Points, Oxford American, North American Review, New England Review, Fiction International, Ecotone, Virginia Quarterly Review, Carolina Quarterly,* and elsewhere. A 2009–10 Guggenheim fellowship recipient, Singleton received the 2011 Hillsdale Award from the Fellowship of Southern Writers and was inducted into the South Carolina Academy of Authors in 2010. He holds the John C. Cobb Endowed Chair in the Humanities at Wofford College in Spartanburg.

KATIE STAGLIANO is founder and CEO of Katie's Krops, a not-for-profit organization that starts and maintains vegetable gardens and donates their harvests to help feed people in need. In 2014 Katie's Krops had more than seventy-five kid-run vegetable gardens in twenty-nine states producing thousands of pounds of healthy and fresh food for families in need. She is the youngest recipient of the Clinton Global Citizenship Award, a Global Teen Leader for the We Are Family Foundation, and a member of the youth advisory board for the Alliance for a Healthier Generation. Honored in 2014 as one of the top ten youth volunteers in the nation with a Prudential Spirit of Community Award, Stagliano has been featured in numerous national publications and broadcasts. Her work was told in *The Starfish Throwers,* an award-winning feature-length film. The author of *Katie's Cabbage,* Stagliano lives in Summerville.

MICHEL SMOAK Stone's debut novel, *The Iguana Tree,* which *Kirkus Reviews* says "recalls the work of John Steinbeck," received a starred review from *Publishers Weekly* and has been lauded for addressing a controversial issue without seeming heavy-handed or political. The author of numerous stories and essays, she is a 2011 recipient of the South Carolina Fiction Project Award awarded by the South Carolina Arts Commission. Stone grew up on Johns Island and lives in Spartanburg with her husband, Eliot, their three children, and her Boykin spaniel. Her second novel is well under way.

MARJORY WENTWORTH'S poems have been nominated for the Pushcart Prize five times. Her books of poetry include *Noticing Eden, Despite Gravity, The Endless Repetition of an Ordinary Miracle,* and *New and Selected Poems.* She is the cowriter with Juan Mendez of *Taking a Stand: The Evolution of Human Rights,* coeditor with Kwame Dawes of *Seeking: Poetry and Prose Inspired by the Art of Jonathan Greene,* and the author of the prizewinning children's story *Shackles.* Marjory is on the faculty at the Colleges of Charleston and the Art Institute of Charleston. She is the cofounder of the Lowcountry Initiative for the Literary Arts. Her work is included in the South Carolina Poetry Archives at Furman University, and she is the Poet Laureate of South Carolina.

ERNEST L. WIGGINS, an associate professor of journalism at the University of South Carolina, moved to Orangeburg from Washington, D.C., when he was ten. It wasn't long before he discovered a fascination with unbeaten paths, which he pursued in the newsrooms of the *State* and *Columbia Record* newspapers, and in state and national forests. Wiggins is the author of a collection of essays and short fiction, *Reflections of a Native Son in the New South* (Red Letter Press, 2009).

SUSAN MILLAR WILLIAMS is the author of *A Devil and a Good Woman, Too: The Lives of Julia Peterkin* and the coauthor, with Stephen G. Hoffius, of *Upheaval in Charleston: Earthquake and Murder on the Eve of Jim Crow.* She teaches writing at Trident Technical College in Charleston.

CURTIS WORTHINGTON is a writer, performer, and physician in Charleston, and the author of occasional articles, critical essays, and literary history. Editor of *Literary Charleston: A Lowcountry Reader* and *Literary Charleston and the Lowcountry,* Worthington is a recipient of the Poetry Society of South Carolina's Skylark Prize.